C000052182

THE MEI

Thousands of British women lived in India during Victorian times. They first went out as wives, mothers, sisters; others followed as teachers, doctors, missionaries. What they did and how they responded to their strange environment were seldom thought worthy of record, and writers have handed down to us a fictional image of the typical 'memsahib' as a frivolous, snobbish and selfish creature flitting from bridge to tennis parties 'in the hills' while her poor husband slaved 'on the plains'. For the most part, these clichés bear little resemblance to the truth; many women loyally and stoically accepted their share of responsibility with endurance, courage and resilience.

This story is developed around a number of women who wrote in an entertaining and intelligent fashion about their Indian experiences, starting with the arrival on the scene of one of the wittiest and cleverest of them all – Emily Eden, sister of Lord Auckland who was Governor-General from 1836 to 1842. It ends with Maud Diver, who maintained that the random assertion made by Kipling about the 'lower tone of social morality' in India was unjust and untrue, though even Mrs Diver admitted it might prevail in Simla. The *dramatis personae* of the book include Vicereines, wives of serving officers, movingly described in the context of the seige at Lucknow, wives of Civil Servants coping with only the rudiments of civilization in up-country stations, missionaries struggling to break down the subservience of women throughout the vast sub-continent. Through women's eyes we witness the principal historic events of the time – the Afghan conflicts, the Mutiny – as well as the daily routines in very different cantonments and some of the British personalities who made their mark on nineteenth-century India – Honoria Lawrence, Flora Steel, Lady Sale. In this vivid account Pat Barr evokes the sights and smells of Victorian India, its teeming masses, it problems so impossible, it seemed, for Englishwomen to solve. It is to the credit of the majority of her characters that they made the attempt.

Pat Barr has already established a reputation for herself as a popular historian with a particular interest in the lives of people in unfamiliar surroundings. Her other books include *The Coming of the Barbarians* and *The Deer Cry Pavilion* about the coming of the Europeans to Japan in the nineteenth century, her biography of the traveller Isabella Bird, *A Curious Life for a Lady*, and *To China with Love*, an account of the Protestant missionaries in China. She has lived in many parts of the world, including the United States, Japan and Bolivia.

THE MEMSAHIBS

*The Women of
Victorian India*

PAT BARR

CENTURY

LONDON SYDNEY AUCKLAND JOHANNESBURG

Copyright © Pat Barr 1976

All rights reserved

First published by Secker & Warburg 1976

This edition published in 1989 by Century,
an imprint of Century Hutchinson Ltd,
Brookmount House, 62–65 Chandos Place,
Covent Garden, London WC2N 4NW

Century Hutchinson Australia Pty Ltd,
89–91 Albion Street, Surry Hills,
Sydney, New South Wales 2010, Australia

Century Hutchinson New Zealand Limited,
PO Box 40–086, Glenfield, Auckland 10,
New Zealand

Century Hutchinson South Africa (Pty) Ltd,
PO Box 337, Bergvlei, 2012 South Africa

Cover painting shows detail from *The Flight from Lucknow* by
Abraham Solomon (courtesy of Museum and Art Gallery of
Leicester)

British Library Cataloguing in Publication Data

Barr, Pat, *1934 –*
  The memsahibs: the women of Victorian India.
  1. India. British women, 1785–1947
  I. Title   II. Series
  954.03

ISBN 0 7126 2561 5

Printed and bound by The Guernsey Press,
Guernsey, Channel Islands

For Jean Lavender
with love

ACKNOWLEDGEMENTS

I should like to express my appreciation for the constructive help I received from Miss Mary Thatcher, archivist of the Centre of South Asian Studies in Cambridge, whose shared enthusiasm for the subject was a great stimulus. I should also like to thank the staff of the India Office Library for their assistance. I am grateful too for the advice and encouragement I received from Mr John Hearsey, Mr Richard Collier and the late Lady Stokes.

CONTENTS

INTRODUCTION

Thousands of British women lived in India during Victorian times. They went out as wives, mothers, sisters; later as teachers, doctors, missionaries. But, because of the social prejudices and conventions of the times, their roles were traditionally supportive and secondary. What they did and how they responded to their alien environment were seldom thought worthy of record, either by themselves or by contemporary chroniclers of the male-dominated imperial scenario. Later historians have blamed them for narrowing and domesticating the British experience of India and for exacerbating the racial prejudice which increasingly divided the rulers from the ruled. Writers, particularly the so well known Rudyard Kipling, have handed down to us a fictional image of the typical 'memsahib' as a frivolous, snobbish and selfish creature who flitted from bridge to tennis parties 'in the hills' while her poor husband slaved 'on the plains'.

These resemblances are historical clichés of little substance. For the most part, the women loyally and stoically accepted their share of the white people's burden and lightened the weight of it with their quiet humour, their grace, and often their youth. For many of them first went to India in their early twenties – eager, shy, curious and brave, though not armed with very much in the way of worldly experience or formal education. Nevertheless, some of them contributed much to the British understanding of India, some suffered harrowing ordeals and very hard times, some put all their energies into worthy causes, some stayed put in up-country stations for years, just making the best of it. All of them were individuals in their own right and faced, as frequently as their male compatriots, situations that demanded all their reserves of endurance, courage and resilience.

I have chosen to develop this story around a number of women who wrote in an entertaining, intelligent and interesting fashion about their Indian experiences, and I have started with the arrival on the scene of one of the wittiest and cleverest of them all – Emily Eden, sister of Lord Auckland, who was Governor-General from 1836 to 1842.

By that time, trading establishments of the East India Company had existed in India for over two hundred years and the divisions of parliamentary and Company power over those areas of the country known as British India had been outlined since 1772, when Warren Hastings was appointed the first Governor-General of Bengal. During the next sixty years a handful of aggressive, dynamic and ambitious men – the Lords Cornwallis, Wellesley, Minto and Bentinck among them – dominated the course of Anglo-Indian affairs, extended the Company's territories and instituted a number of political and social reforms. As more men came out from Britain to keep military order, administrate and trade in the expanding Empire, they formed an ostentatious pleasure-and-money-seeking community, centred chiefly on Calcutta. More women came too – though they were still a small minority – and they too were notorious for their indolent and lavish life-style.

Things were changing by the 1830s: a new sober spirit of dutiful imperialism allied to crusading evangelicism was abroad which was to become an overriding influence during the course of Queen Victoria's long reign. The Eden sisters were, of course, pre-Victorian by background and temperament; the young queen, who came to the throne of England the year after they reached India, was, to Emily Eden, a 'charming invention'. As an 'invention', Victoria was most effective – especially when, in 1876, Disraeli invented for her the title 'Empress of India' and she became, for both Anglo-Indians and Indians, a symbol of the power and prosperity of the British Empire overseas.

Of that Empire, Michael Edwardes, a modern authority on Indian affairs, has written that it 'was constructed out of individual sacrifice, not the incandescent sacrifice of the battlefield, nor the conscious hand-on-heart, all-for-England sacrifice of the comfortable propagandists back home, but the commonplace, almost casual acceptance of discomfort, boredom and death. It is easy, almost inevitable, to dislike the great names of British India, to be revolted at their cruelties, their indifference and their shallow minds. But for those unknowns who really made the Empire, the soldiers, clerks and the women who lived and died and were forgotten, it is possible only to feel pity.' Not only pity surely, also a certain measure of respect, affection and understanding that is always aroused when one starts to read between the lines of any great human adventure.

PART ONE

Chapter One

The summer of 1834 was hot by English standards – that is by the standards of English people like Emily and Fanny Eden who neither had nor wanted any direct experience of tropical heat. To escape the stuffiness of crowded London therefore, the two women, who were the unmarried sisters of the unmarried George, Lord Auckland, took a cottage at Ham Common, near Richmond. They were still staying there in October when, one cool autumnal evening, Emily sat down to write to her friend, Theresa Lister. They were leaving the cottage in two days, she told Theresa, and going to Admiralty House where George, who was First Lord of the Admiralty in Lord Melbourne's Whig Government, was living alone; they had to go and keep him company 'till the Government changes or I am ill again'. For the Whig hold on the country was tenuous and George's position uncertain, which made Emily want to be near him, for brother and sister were close companions and turned to each other in time of stress.

At the end of the letter Emily wrote, 'There was a great sough of India for about a fortnight but I always held it was too bad to be true, which is a dangerous assertion to make in many cases, it only hastens the catastrophe. But this was such an extreme case, such a horrible supposition, that there was nothing for it but to bully it; and the danger is now over. Botany Bay would be a joke to it. There is a decent climate to begin with and the fun of a little felony first. But to be sent to Calcutta for no cause at all! At all events, I should hardly have got there before George got home again, for I should have walked across the country to join him, if

I had gone at all. I think I see myself going into a ship for five months! I would not do it for a £1000 per day.'

In October 1835, Lord Auckland, the newly appointed Governor-General of India, left Portsmouth on a sailing ship called the *Jupiter* to take up his duties; he was accompanied by his two sisters, Emily and Fanny, his nephew, William Osborne, and their pet dog, Chance. Five months later, on 4th March 1836 (which happened to be Emily's thirty-ninth birthday, though everyone except herself was too preoccupied to remember it), the *Jupiter* reached Calcutta. In her first letter to Theresa, from Government House, Emily wrote, 'We have been here three weeks and are so accustomed to our way of life that I cannot help thinking we have been here much longer and that it is nearly time to go home again.'

They were to spend six years in India, during which time Emily never ceased wanting to go home again. It was by far the most eventful and exciting period of her life, but she did not require excitement to make her happy. What brought her true joy was the society of her close family and dearest friends, the cool beauties of the English countryside and the charms of Park Lodge, Greenwich, where she, George and Fanny had been living in the good old days, when her brother was simply a Commissioner of Greenwich Hospital, and the furthest she had to travel was up to town, or to Chatsworth to stay with the Duke of Devonshire, or to Kent and Essex to visit her married sisters.

Then, in early 1834, had come George's Admiralty appointment which had meant leaving Greenwich altogether; then the Whig Government had fallen as Emily had predicted, and there had followed months of insecurity for the sisters while the politicians made up their minds who was to rule the country. In April 1835, when the Whigs were returned to Westminster, Emily's 'horrible supposition' became a reality: Auckland was 'given India'. It was a position that carried with it a great deal of prestige, a high salary and supreme administrative authority over the British Presidencies of Bengal, Madras and Bombay. In India George was directly answerable to no one; but he had two masters in England – the Whig Government and the Directors of the East India Company. In matters of political policy he was to act in consultation with the

Home Government whenever possible; in commercial matters he was responsible to 'The Company'.

It was not an easy assignment, made less so in George's case because his predecessor, Lord William Bentinck, had instituted a number of successful and far-reaching social and legal reforms which Auckland was expected to consolidate and extend. At his farewell banquet in London, given by the Court of the East India Company Directors, Lord Auckland had welcomed such an opportunity for 'doing good to his fellow creatures, of promoting education and knowledge, of improving administration and justice in India and of extending the blessing of good government and happiness to millions of her people'. And doubtless he did go to Calcutta with the best intentions; he was considered able, with an unflappable disposition and a strong head for hard work. But he lacked imagination, flexibility and sound personal judgement. His sisters possessed some of these qualities, but they were not in India to govern; they were there as the very top memsahibs of the country and their functions were social, decorative and ceremonial.

'We have great dinners of fifty people,' wrote Emily to Theresa of her initial experiences. 'Visiting time at Government House is from ten to one in the mornings, and we found it so fatiguing to have a hundred or a hundred and fifty people at that time of day we have now chosen Tuesday evenings and Thursday mornings and we do not mean to be at home the rest of the week.' It was all very formal and very tiresome. Everyone passing through Calcutta felt they had to call at Government House – and everyone *was* always passing through. 'They come to Calcutta on their way out to make their fortunes or on their way home because they have made them, or because their healths require a change of station and they come here to ask for it,' Emily explained. 'They look very smart, come in immense numbers, sit down for five minutes and, if there are forty in the room at once, never speak to each other.' That was to be a constant burden of complaint – the numbers of strangers she had to entertain, while those whose company she most desired were either thousands of miles away or surrounded, as she was, by the undesired. 'I never see G. at Calcutta except in a crowd,' she mourned – so thank goodness for the house at Barrackpore, where she was able to take elephant rides with him alone.

Barrackpore was their weekend retreat, a fairly modest establishment by gubernatorial standards, standing in a large park by the River Ganges, sixteen miles from Calcutta. It was somewhat shabby, its furniture 'worse than that of any London hotel', its gardens and menagerie long neglected, but both Fanny and Emily loved it at once. 'Certainly the place to live at,' decided Fanny. 'In short, Barrackpore is, I see, to save me from India,' wrote Emily. 'A charming place, like a beautiful English villa on the banks of the Thames – so green and fresh.' Moreover, it 'only holds three', by which she meant that the Governor's aides and all the tiresome visitors were accommodated in thatched bungalows dotted round the park. And, to remind one more of Home, the park even had little hills in it, which, said Fanny, 'rose in the days when Lord Hastings said, "Make a hill", and one was made'.

The unquestioning and prompt fulfilment of their every wish which resulted from their elevated status was a trifle startling at first, even to those of the Edens' aristocratic background. 'The subserviency of the natives to the handful of white men who have got into this country shocks me at this moment,' wrote Fanny, after being there four days. And Emily asked another of her close friends, Lady Pamela Campbell, 'It seems so odd to have everything one wants, doesn't it, Pam? I wanted a vase for fish in my garden; the civil engineer immediately put up two.' Other improvements of the Barrackpore establishment were put in train with a wave of the hand: a secluded private garden filled with familiar English flora to remind them of dear Greenwich; the menagerie filled with the strange fauna of the country – cheetahs, sloths, porcupines, black pheasants and white monkeys.

For Emily the best times of all at Barrackpore were when she and George 'rode up and down by the waterside on the elephant . . . There is something dreamy and odd in these rides when the evening grows dark. There is a mosque and a ghaut at the end of our park where they were burning a body tonight; and there were bats, as big as crows, flying over our heads. The river was covered with odd-looking boats, and a red copper-coloured sky bent over all.' And the pair of them must have looked quite odd too – upright in their howdahs against the coloured sky, the disdainful Eden nose atwitch with the smell of burning flesh. When they returned, to lounge in the verandah after dinner and play familiar games like chess or *écarte*, fireflies spun by in the dark and in the distance jackals barked. They could not easily adjust to so much strangeness, their Indian existence 'more like a constant theatrical representation going on, everything is so picturesque and utterly un-English'.

At Barrackpore the picturesqueness was a compensation, but as for Calcutta, 'it is all very magnificent but I cannot endure our life there', Emily decided, though she had to. They returned to Government House every Sunday evening for five days of social and ceremonial functions, where they met hundreds of people, but from among whom they plucked no new friends. Asked by Theresa if she had come across any 'pleasing or accomplished women', Emily replied, 'Not one – not a sixth part of one; there is not anybody I can prefer to any other body. They read no new books, they take not the slightest interest in home politics and everything is melted down to the purely local.'

Anglo-Indian society in Calcutta had been notorious for this narrow parochialism since the late seventeenth century when the first overseas trading houses were established there. The increasing wealth of the foreign community was based entirely on commerce and its aspirations on the lifestyle of the eighteenth-century British nabob. The nabobs were famed for the size and extravagance of their households, their gargantuan appetites and the numbers of their 'dusky mistresses'. For in those days English women were indeed a rarity in India and those there were not, in the opinion of one male resident, 'either in the education of intellect or heart what an intelligent, reflecting and cultivated man would select as his companion'. Not that the ladies were short of admirers. Sophia Goldbourne, one of the fair few, wrote home that 'the attention and court paid to me was astonishing. My smile was meaning and my articulation melody; in a word, mirrors are almost useless in Calcutta and self-adoration idle, for your looks are reflected in the pleasures of every beholder and your claims to first-rate distinction confirmed by all who approach you.'

By the early nineteenth century more English ladies had arrived on the scene, and in the rows of mansions at Chowringhee, Calcutta's richest quarter, no expense was spared to re-create for them the ambience of luxurious western-style comfort. Their lofty rooms were stuffed with 'objects your only interest in which would arise from their familiar associations', wrote the anonymous author of the *Anglo-Indian Domestic Sketch Book*. They boasted 'marble halls and passages, carpeted floors, oil-clothed stairs, fireplaces with all their decorative accompaniments, window curtains, chandeliers, stained glass and, in short, a thousand and one ornamental elegances of fashionable life that would do no discredit to St James'.

No matter that these mansions were built upon a noisome swamp, along filthy streets near the river where corpses of people and animals bobbed up to be torn apart by vultures and alligators. That, after all, was always India . . . and even inside these sumptuous establishments, the country made its presence felt. Legs of furniture stood in saucers of water to minimize destruction by white ants; cups and glasses were topped with horn covers to keep out flying insects; green gauze mosquito-nets shrouded the large mahogany bedsteads. The thick frills of the punkahs suspended from the ceiling were kept in continuous motion by coolies who sat on the verandahs outside and pulled their attaching ropes; but the slow, creaking swish of the moving cloth induced its own languor, and ladies tended to remain fixed to the same square of carpet for hours, waiting for the next breath of air to arrive. When it did so, however, one's curls were dreadfully ruffled, and what with that, and the hazards of insect bites, heat rashes and the rapid mildewing of silks and satins in the rainy season, it was almost impossible to look truly elegant for long in India.

Another way of trying at least to look cool was to stand near the tatties, which were screens of dried grass placed before open doors and windows. When the searingly hot winds blew, coolies kept the tatties constantly wet, the idea being that the entering blasts would be thus transformed into damp English-sea-like breezes. When there was no wind, therm-antidotes were put next to the tatties to create one. They were large wooden cases enclosed on three sides and containing an arrangement of fans on a central wheel, rather like a winnowing machine, and turned by a large iron handle. Butter and milk kept fresh a few hours longer if stored inside them, but their effect on people was not spectacularly cooling. Nothing was. 'It is so very HOT, I do not know how to spell it large enough,' Emily told Pamela.

People unused to such temperatures do very little in them unless forced. The men, who had to earn enough money to bring in the butter and keep the punkahs moving, managed to continue work; the women, for whom there was little compulsion to do anything much, often lapsed into inertia and dullness. 'In her drawing-room for the chief part of her day, the Anglo-Indian lady is as much a prisoner by reason of the heat as the zenana woman is by custom,' wrote one sympathetic gentleman. 'She is by herself all day long and thrown on her own resources of music, reading, letter-writing or sketching.'

Alone and yet not freely alone, for at every turn servants waited to do her every bidding and encourage her indolence. Top of the service hierarchy indoors were the butlers and footmen (who wore household liveries), the cooks, valets for the gentlemen, ayahs, amahs and wet nurses for the ladies and children. Each person of consequence had his own tailor who sat cross-legged snipping and sewing on the verandah all day, and most of them had personal dhobies, washermen who arrived in the mornings on a donkey laden with equipment – soap board, a stick for thrashing clothes clean, drying lines and a firebox for heating the water. The water was carried by a bhistie who had also to fill the rows of earthenware jars in the bathrooms and keep the tatties wet. Then there were the general domestics who carried messages or goods, cleaned and swept, filled and trimmed the lamps. And outside in the gardens and compound was another structure of service, topped by the coachmen, elephant-drivers (mahouts) and head-gardeners, through the fowlkeepers, cowmen, grooms, watch-men, palanquin-bearers, grass-cutters and gatekeepers, and down to the young lads who swept the stables, cleaned the latrines and the wells, and dug the irrigation ditches round the vegetable plots.

As a lady newly arrived in Madras commented, the result of such a system was that 'Every creature seems eaten up with laziness. Even my horse pretends he is too fine to switch off his own flies with his own long tail, but turns his head round to order the horsekeepers to wipe them off for him.' It was a commonplace that, in the British establishments, the servants were often treated worse than the animals. Emily Eden mentions that the natives competed for employment at Government House because it was 'one of the few houses in Calcutta where they are not beaten. It is quite horrible and disgusting to see how people quietly let out that that they are in the habit of beating these timid, weak creatures.' But the servants were so poor they had to bear it, and the English, even had they wished for less grandeur, could not economize by letting one servant perform several tasks because of the taboos of the caste system. And so, after being in the country a short time, Emily admitted that the Edens, like everyone else, were 'gradually acquiring the Indian habit of denying ourselves nothing'.

The Edens, while learning to adapt themselves to the extrava-gancies and deprivations of their new life, were also able to stand apart from it, strong in the knowledge that it could not last for more than six years at the worst and that everything back home afterwards would be pleasurable by comparison ... Assuming, of course, one was lucky and lived long enough to return home, for there was no denying that the India of the period was a dangerous place for foreigners and an alarming number of men and women under forty died there of fevers and other undiagnosed illnesses.

After their first visit to the burial ground at Barrackpore, Emily wrote home with determined cheerfulness, 'We are much too old to die in India evidently, so do not be alarmed about us.' On the same subject, she adds, 'You cannot imagine in India how the ranks close in the very day after a death. The most intimate friends never stay at home above two days and they see everybody again directly. It is a constant surprise to me, but I suppose there is some good reason for it.' The reason probably was that the very frequency of death meant that it had to be taken fairly easily in stride; if the rituals of mourning had been too elaborate and long, society would never have been free of them. But the Edens were fortunate; in spite of various 'spasms' and unhealthy-looking complexions of a 'delicate tender sun-baked yellow', they all kept remarkably fit.

By the spring of their second year Fanny felt so acclimatized and energetic that she resolved to go on a tiger-hunting expedition with her nephew William Osborne, whose company she greatly enjoyed. George and Emily were so closely, if coolly, attuned that the younger sister must always have felt something of a third party in the household. So it was lucky that, in India, she had the special friendship of William – a high-spirited, nonchalant young man who enjoyed simple pleasures like smoking a hookah, camping, riding and shooting. At that time the mofussil (countryside) teemed with things to shoot: peacocks (whose screeches held 'a sound of home' for Fanny), deer, alligators, snipe, rhinoceros, partridges and wild hogs which came bounding out of jungles aflare with wild roses.

The party rode elephant-back through the hills and 'the gentlemen have with them each six rifles and shoot at all innocent beasts and birds they meet,' Fanny explained. She played it for laughs, as was the family habit. Settled one afternoon to write letters on the bank of a river, in advance of the masculine contingent who were 'shooting their way here', she suddenly saw a head poking about the surface of the water nearby. It looked like a harmless otter's, but belonged to an alligator. 'I am very fond of alligators,' she wrote immediately in her letter. 'I say that to please it.' There were, she then realized, three more snoozing on the opposite bank: 'Not make-believe beasts at all, but eighteen or twenty feet long. I have nothing but Mrs C's little lap dog to offer them in exchange for myself.'

The gentlemen acquired a respectable number of tiger-skins in due course; she settled for one live spotted deer. It was a devoted creature which travelled in her howdah, trotted behind her like a dog and ate delicately from its own cup and saucer. Fanny, who had a more open-air and relaxed temperament than Emily, gloried in the beauteous freedoms of camp life and dreaded the return to 'that great, hot, shut-up prison of a palace' called Government House. Nor did she appear to miss George and Emily very much. The former, she mentioned, 'was growing very despotic when I left home; he may have committed any atrocity during our absence – he has probably cut off the heads of all the aides-de-camp'. It was the sort of thing he might have enjoyed had he been a true eastern potentate, for one senses a certain cold callousness about George, from which only his close relations were exempt.

'Lord Auckland has a very dry manner always. The sisters quite the reverse, extremely agreeable,' wrote Mary Wimberley, after her first dinner at the Governor's residence in Barrackpore, which took place while Fanny was away on her up-country jaunt. Mary had the chance of observing the Governor-General closely on that occasion because, as she explained, he 'handed me to table as there was no greater lady'. She had no pretensions to great lady-liness, being quite happy as the wife of Charles Wimberley, who had recently become his Lordship's private chaplain.

The Wimberleys had spent the past twelve years shifting about the world in the Christian cause and, compared to where they had been, their 'nice clean little cottage' in Barrackpore park seemed a haven of comfort. They had first been assigned to India in 1826, then to the Straits Settlements at Malacca, then Java, Macao, Cape Town and back to Fort William, Calcutta, where they lived in four small stifling rooms with no running water, no nursery and no stabling for their horse and buggy. Mary was a Scot, with the national characteristic of resilient practicality which she greatly needed, having married a man whose principal gift was for pulpit oratory, and having already borne him five children in various uncongenial habitations. However it was her husband's power of preaching in a manner sufficiently stirring to entice people to worship even in the heat of Sunday mid-mornings that had resulted in his Barrackpore appointment.

'We had a good sermon on Good Friday and another today,' wrote Emily of Wimberley's first Easter services; which was praise indeed, for Miss Eden was a connoisseur of sermons. 'But the heat at the altar was beyond anything; there was no punkah there and no glass windows in this church, so the hot air came pouring in as if we were in an oven'. Mary did not mind too much about the heat on that occasion because she was happy to see the large congregation and that it yielded a total of 156 rupees in the collection box – fifty of them from Lord Auckland himself. Naturally therefore the Wimberleys took good care not to offend the Governor-General and his sisters – though this meant accepting invitations to dine with them on a Sunday, which was against Charles' principles, but, as Mary realistically put it, 'one cannot well refuse "My Lord"'.

When the Top Family were away in Calcutta during the week, the permanent Barrackpore residents arranged jolly, informal musical evenings, during which Mrs Littler played the harp divinely, Mary recorded in her journal. Captain Andrews did his best on the viola, though its upper registers were dreadfully squeaky; Mrs Abbot would insist on singing 'as if bawling were melody'. The park was another delight to Mary – the watered lawns almost English-green, parakeets chattering in the tamarind trees, and visits with Baby Henry, her youngest child, to the tiger cubs in the menagerie and the goldfish in the huge lily-covered ornamental tanks.

But poor Baby Henry did not flourish. He had 'tooth rash on his feet', bowel trouble, blisters behind his ears. The doctor's only remedy was to keep lancing the infant's gums to bring through his eye teeth, whose non-appearance was thought to be the cause of the trouble. The treatment was not effective and in the summer Henry died, his gums still bleeding. It was a great blow to the Wimberleys who felt 'so very unhappy and perplexed about whether we dare keep our other dear children in this sad country'. It was a problem that beset most Anglo–Indian parents and there were few who did not, sooner or later, suffer the loss of at least one child.

For the Edens, none of whom, incidentally, seem to have ever contemplated seriously any marital and parental involvements, it was a reasonably pleasant summer. Fanny returned 'looking uncommonly well, in prodigious spirits and quite *brushed up* by her expedition', her elder sister reported. George was in danger of getting fat and his hair was going white, but his vigour seemed unimpaired. 'I really feel every day that I could not be away from G.,' Emily wrote. 'He could not have existed here alone and for want of other colleagues I can see constantly that it is a great comfort to have me to talk over his little bothers with.'

It was true; she was essential to his equilibrium, and when Lord Auckland began to plan an extensive tour of the north-west provinces, it was taken for granted that his sisters should accompany him, though it was unusual for ladies of such elevated status to take long journeys 'up-country'. None of the Edens was very keen on the project, but it would provide a change of scenery and, hopefully, impress the natives. As Emily put it, 'our first and best energies are devoted towards making a *clinquant* figure of His Excellency, in order that he may shine in the eyes of the native princes; and I take it he will make a pretty considerable figure seen through a long vista of embroidered punkahs, peacock feathers, silver sticks, spearmen etc. and two interesting females caracoling on their elephants on each side of him.'

From George's point of view, it was essential that he gain some first-hand experience of the real India, for he was surrounded by advisers who knew much more about it than he did and who were full of bushy-tailed ideas about expanding British influence and authority to the various provinces of the north-west. But for the Edens, who had so far been content to float within the official and social circles of Calcutta and Barrackpore, the rest of the country remained a rather comic unreality. As Fanny expressed it in a July letter to a friend, 'My dear, the King of Oudh is dead! I think I see you start and at once embrace all the political importance of such an event. Then, rousing yourself from mightier thoughts, you will rush to order your Court mourning. We talk of it mysteriously, because we talk of all Indian affairs mysteriously.' Such patronizing flippancy is scarcely excusable and certainly not from George who was nevertheless also prone to it.

But George possessed a too highly developed sense of duty not to go and take a good look at the country under his governorship. Perhaps by so doing he could reassure himself that it would get along all right without too much intervention on his part in the future, for neither he nor his sisters had any urgent desire to probe very deeply into the mysteries of Indian affairs.

Chapter Two

There were rumours in August that the Whigs would lose power in which case Lord Auckland would have to go home to Kensington instead of on his planned tour Up the Country, on which the Wimberleys were to accompany him. Most of the ladies concerned, including Emily Eden and Mary Wimberley, devoutly and secretly hoped for such an outcome, but it was not to be. Lord Melbourne, who had appointed 'G.' to the Governor-Generalship, remained at Westminster and so, at Barrackpore, Mary Wimberley had to thrust the sorrow of the baby's death behind her and begin packing. Chaplains, even gubernatorial ones, were expected to make their own transport arrangements. So the Wimberleys sold their small carriage, two of their horses, and packed the rest of their belongings in large wooden chests which were loaded on their baggage-boat moored on the Ganges. They travelled on a budgerow, a flat combination of houseboat and barge; there was another boat for the horses – and poultry to be killed and eaten on route.

Despite being seasoned travellers the Wimberleys were always sadly disaster-prone, and soon after leaving Barrackpore – with every wind in India set against them – the 'miserable broken-down horseboat' nearly sank and the rudder fell off the baggage-boat. Then their principal syce decamped because Charles Wimberley 'would not let him keep his bad woman in the Horse Boat' (even though she did the cooking), and when they reached Patna their budgerow filled with water, though luckily they were ashore at the time. So great were their trials and delays – Charles 'perpetually at loggerheads' with the servants over their morals and their pay, and 'rushing about the whole day in the Sun and Moon trying to get the apathetic wretches to do things' – that, come troubled Monday morning, Mary was 'perfectly astonished to find that yesterday was Sunday'. It was, however, a very special case for dispensation because, by now, Mary was terrified lest 'we shall not be at Benares in time to meet the Governor-General . . . and then *what* shall we do?'

Lord Auckland and his sisters had left Calcutta on 21st October 'for eighteen months of travelling by steamers, tents and mountains' Emily wrote inconsequentially, hating the prospect ahead because 'every day of a cabin seems like so much of waste'. For, if Mary Wimberley was an unlucky traveller, Emily Eden was a reluctant one, and she begins her account of the Governor-General's Grand Processional across India by confessing that the whole exercise was a dreadful chore 'for a person who required nothing but to be allowed the undisturbed enjoyment of that small Greenwich home and garden with all its little cockney pleasures and pursuits'.

And, at first, it all proved as dispiriting and uncomfortable as she had anticipated. They glided slowly up the Ganges on 'flats' which were spacious barges towed by steamers; the surrounding countryside was equally flat, its most remarkable feature being the occasional 'bamboo stuck up with a bush tied to it to recall the cheerful fact that there a tiger has carried off a man'; G. was bored stiff within two days and longing for the comparative cool of Government House; they could not sleep a wink because of the furnace-like heat and the numbers of servants who lay about 'everywhere, over our heads, under our feet or at our doors' and coughed and spat the whole night through.

With all the pauses en route for visiting out-stations, sketching ruins and holding durbars, it took them three weeks to reach Benares – which the Wimberleys had thankfully attained just thirty-six hours before, quite 'ill and exhausted by the constant state of excitement and anxiety', Mary explained. But now she could relax, for she was among the comparatively privileged members of the Imperial Cavalcade. It was twelve thousand strong: with governmental secretaries and scribes, aides-de-camp, army officers and their wives and children; soldiers, sepoys, servants and servants' servants; drivers, drummers and valets, guards and guards' guards; laundrymen and loaders, messengers and tent-pitchers, grass-cutters and cooks; and mahouts and amahs and herders and grooms. To transport this multitude and their equipment between ten and twenty miles a day overland in strictly hierarchical degrees of comfort required unspecified numbers of elephants, oxen, camels, horses and ponies; tilburies, buggies and jonpauns (sedan chairs on poles carried by four bearers); hackeries drawn by bullocks, palanquins that were furnished with shelves, a little oil lamp and a mosquito net, rather like a steamer-berth, and dhoolies, covered litters lighter and cheaper than palanquins and described by one traveller as 'a tray for women' and by another as 'little four-poster beds with very short legs and curtains buttoned up all round to keep out the rain'.

The overland journey began at Benares where they all took to tents. 'The Governor-General's tents are splendid and our own most comfortable looking,' wrote Mary Wimberley, mindful of all the worse berths she had known. And indeed a prodigal quantity of canvas was used to protect the Eden heads from the excesses of the climate. They each had a private tent with its own bedroom, dressing-room, sitting-room and these were connected to each other by wide covered passages and to another communal sitting-room; opposite this extensive private enclosure were two vast tents – for dining and durbaring. But for Emily it was still 'open-airish and unsafe', with walls that flapped uneasily and floors that tended to sink; 'I had never seen such squalid, melancholy discomfort,' she decided. And George agreed with her of course, brother and elder sister at one in their distastes as in their disdains. Emily named her tent Misery Hall; George called his Foully Palace; Fanny said it was odd as 'everyone observed that *her* tent was like a fairy palace'.

The Wimberleys lived in a humbler abode known as The Vicarage and on Sundays, when the whole camp halted, Charles preached Divine Service in the Durbar Tent that was arranged quite 'like a chapel' for the occasion. But it was not really a chapel, much less a church than the dear, cool stone one in Greenwich that Emily remembered so well, and the 'streets' that were laid out in front of the principal tents at every halt were not proper thoroughfares with sounds of muffin-men and horses' hooves; and the country they were so laboriously traversing was just an endlessly drear plain, on which a mosque ballooned here and there, but 'nothing really to give a name to'.

Nevertheless this seemingly empty desert pulsated with those who had names which they were determined to impress upon the off-hand and irritable Lord Auckland. 'The usual assortment of magistrates, judges, collectors, etc,' Emily noted, who carted him off to inspect their new jails, roads and court-rooms; the leading ladies and gentlemen of each and every out-station who travelled miles and stood in perspiring lines to exchange a few, hopefully memorable, pleasantries with the Governor's party. But however amiably Emily Eden might have contrived to fix her official smile, she nurtured fairly low opinions of Anglo–Indians. So parochial and out of date did she find their conversation that she usually commanded the band to play at dinners, in order to fill in awkward pauses and drown what chat there was.

The large stations were therefore the worst to cope with – Cawnpore, for instance, which they all detested. There was famine in the district, so the skeletons at the feasts were closer than usual and, in the nearby villages, 'the women's skulls look dreadful'. Mary Wimberley had never seen such a place 'for Dust and Mud Walls'. 'Dreadful,' agreed Emily and, worst of all, so many people that 'there is not a chance of getting through all our duties if we lose an hour's time'. So they started at once with a levee, followed by a dance and party in the large tent that held three hundred. Next morning, some local rajahs came to breakfast, Emily and Fanny received the ladies between eleven o'clock and one, and that evening there was a regimental dinner for seventy-five. The dinners were the worst, endless at the end of an endless day, with up to half-hour waits between courses. At one such, Emily wrote home, 'I quite lost my head and, when the second course was put down, asked Mr T. . . . to give me some wine, thinking it was dessert and that we might get up and go.' But in spite of all the social efforts made, few ever succeeded in their jostles for recognition. Cawnpore, Emily decided, was 'one of those crowded stations where it is better not to fatigue a failing memory by any attempt at names'.

After several days of these hectic rounds, it was time to move on – bugle-call at 5.30 a.m. and the Edens among the first to take the road because no one of any consequence was allowed to precede them. This had its advantages because it meant they escaped the ever-thickening clouds of dust that smothered the procession's tail, but it did mean starting very early indeed. 'I get such fits of bore with being doddled about for three hours before breakfast in a sedan chair,' Emily wrote, 'that I have a sort of mad wish to tell the bearers to turn back and go home, quite home, all the way to England.'

Behind the First Family rode other leading members of the entourage: Mr Macnaghten, Lord Auckland's political secretary, and his wife who rode in a very smart carriage, Major Byrne's wife in a palanquin with her pet cat and her ayah opposite, guarding her pet parakeet from the cat, and of course the Wimberleys who were as unlucky on land as on water. Soon after they left Benares a mutinous camel threw their entire stock of crockery off his back and trampled on it and, from then on, Emily noticed, 'whether the road be good or bad they always come to a misfortune . . . Yesterday they broke a spring of their dickey; today they had to harness an elephant to their carriage to pull it out of the sand; and soon after we had breakfast we saw the eldest boy arrive on foot, with one of Mrs A's . . . attendants, Mrs Wimberley and the little thing on one of our elephants and Wimberley on his own box, flourishing on with his tired horses.'

The immense quantities of time and effort expended in the covering of such small distances presented to Emily a daily spectacle of splendid absurdity that brought out her richest humour. 'We feel so certain that people who live in houses and get up by a fire at a reasonable hour and then go quietly to break-fast would think us raving mad if they saw nine Europeans of steady age and respectable habits going galloping every morning at sunrise over a sandy plain followed by quantities of black horsemen and then by ten miles of beasts of burden carrying things which, after all, will not make the nine madmen even decently comfortable.' But Emily set extremely high standards in the matter of comfort and certainly every effort was made to reproduce in the alien environment some similitude of dear Home. The burdened beasts carried tables, chairs, cupboards, beds, cushions, mats, dressing-cases and trunks filled with books, linen and tableware which were all arranged in the tents before luncheon each day. In the afternoon, the gentlemen did a little hunting, the ladies a little sketching if it was not too hot and at five o'clock the band was called upon to provide some nostalgic airs so that everyone could promenade 'up and down what we call the High Street in front of our tents', pretending they were back in Calcutta, or, better yet, Lyme Regis.

Their first camp wedding took place just before Christmas between a young writer in the Company's employ and one Miss Sneyd, a specially fortunate occurrence for her, Emily felt, because she had so little money of her own and no relations left in England. The occasion put Charles Wimberley in his usual flurry, 'prancing up and down the tent trying to devise a suitable altar'. Emily suggested he try adapting the scarlet and gold housings of the state elephant. Overriding his doubts about such proximity of the secular and the religious, she sent for them and, with the addition of four armchairs, some carpets and velvet cushions in front 'you can't imagine what a fine altar we made'. Soon after came the next ceremony – Christmas, when the servants hung garlands on all the canvas flaps and Wimberley conducted the Morning Service in his admirable fashion, but 'still it was in a tent and unnatural'. It was all unnatural – sounds of Hindustani voices, sun instead of snow, having to eat various messy concoctions with the heir apparent of Lucknow who was visiting them.

'I am particularly, *Indianly* low today,' Emily recorded that Christmas afternoon, then cheered herself with the thought that it signalled the end of 1837 and so less time before she could leave this draining country 'where everybody looks more than fifty'. India made the men wizen-grey and the women wizen-yellow; it dulled the eyes, the appetite, the wit; it sapped the oil of the skin, the spring of the hair, the vigour of the limb. Seeing those around her to whom this had happened, she was constantly reminded of a verse of George Crabbe's:

> But when returned the youth?
> The youth no more
> Returned exulting to his native shore;
> But in his stead there came a worn-out man.

Emily was forty that year; she desperately wanted to live to see Greenwich again, but if she did, 'please to remember,' she wrote to a friend, 'that I shall return a worn-out woman.'

About this time the Auckland entourage was joined by a lady of a very different stamp, whom India had not worn out, had instead exhilarated, and whose joyous exploration of the wild and wonderful oriental world jumps off the pages of her voluminous *Wanderings of a Pilgrim in Search of the Picturesque*. Her name was Fanny Parkes, who was not precisely a pilgrim but the wife of a customs collector who, during her many years in India, always refused to be the conventional memsahib. 'How weary and heavy is life in India when stationary,' she wrote. 'Travelling about the country is very amusing; but during the heat of the rains, shut up in the house, one's mind and body feel equally enervated.' So, whenever the rains stopped, she left her husband working and took to wandering – by camel, boat, horse, to the north, east and west. Once on the move everything interested her – the construction of the timber rafts poled down to Calcutta by wild black men from the hills, the exploits of the Hindu pantheon, the method of making soap from hill-moss and barley meal, the markings of the rare long-tailed black butterfly; and she entered with zest into whatever was going on – hog-hunting, exploring ruins, climbing into the Himalayas.

However Mrs Parkes had the born traveller's habit of popping in and out of people's lives in an unpredictable and unabashed fashion which irritated some. 'We are rather oppressed just now by a lady, Mrs Parkes, who insists upon belonging to the camp,' wrote Fanny Eden. 'She has entirely succeeded in proving that the

Governor-General's power is but a name . . . The magistrate of one station always travels on with us to the next. To each of these magistrates she has severally attached herself, every successive one declaring they will have nothing to do with her. Upon which G. observes with much complacency, "Now we have got rid of our Mrs P." – and the next morning there she is, on the march, her fresh victim driving her in a tilbury and her tent pitched close to his.'

Fanny Parkes did not see it in the same light. After all, when she had first 'made her salaams' to the Misses Eden they had asked her to dine, had been glad to use her services as an interpreter on their visit to a reigning ranee (for she spoke fluent Hindustani in addition to her other accomplishments). And considering that, as she wrote, the country around the Governor-General's camp was always 'swarming with robbers', it was but prudent to accept offers of protection from various kind military and civilian gentlemen who seemed to enjoy her lively company. Or so she assumed, but to those in the top tents she soon became a figure of fun. Fanny Eden reported home, 'I am sure you will be pleased to know that yesterday, as we were returning from some ruins, G. said, "Here come MacIntosh and Colvin on an elephant. How fat Colvin grows!" Colvin turned out to be Mrs Parkes in a man's hat and riding habit. She had met Captain MacIntosh and, as far as we can make out, climbed up the elephant's tail into his howdah when least expected. She will certainly be the death of us all.'

But the impervious Fanny Parkes continued to jolly along with them, thoroughly enjoying the 'animated and beautiful scenes' of camp life. It was convenient too, for, when they reached the Ganges again, she could cross it on the 'bridge of boats erected for the accommodation of the Lord Sahib, as the natives call the Governor-General . . . They say,' she continued, 'there are about eleven thousand people with the camp, and elephants and camels innumerable, which, added to the Body Guard, Artillery and Infantry, form an immense multitude. It is said his Lordship's marching about the country costs the Government 70,000 rupees a month; the encampment encroaching on fields of grain often costs from 300 to 400 rupees a day to make up the loss sustained by the peasants.'

The Eden sisters do not mention such details, but did record that, after the fatiguing day of crossing the Ganges, Mrs Parkes arrived in camp to find that her servants had pitched her tents inside the gubernatorial sentry-lines. The next morning she received a very stiff note about it from one of the aides-de-camp and, in a state of some huff, took off in a different direction with her friend, the Resident of Gwalior, noting as she did so that 'the formality of the great camp I had just quitted formed a strong contrast to the gaiety and cheerfulness of marching under his flag'.

So she jogged on her way, with her double set of tents, two buggy horses, two arabs, ten camels for the baggage and two bullock carts 'for the women'. In mid-February she was camping on the plains between Meerut and Delhi and, on one particularly splendid morning, wrote in her journal, 'How much there is to delight the eye in this bright, this beautiful world! Roaming about with a good tent and a good arab, one might be happy for ever in India. A man might possibly enjoy this sort of life more than a woman; he has his dog, his gun and his beaters, with an open country to shoot over . . . I have a pencil instead of a gun, and believe it affords me satisfaction equal, if not greater, than the sportsman derives from his Manton.' A great lady, Fanny Parkes, in her fashion, and a pity that, to the Edens, she was not enough of a 'lady' for them to appreciate her sterling qualities.

This is a particular pity as most of the memsahibs Emily met seem to have been very drear – perhaps it was just that she re-served some of her most scathing and snobbish comments for the poor peripheral ladies who had perforce to dance attendance on the Governor-General's party. There was Mrs T . . . who wore thick thread mittens with black velvet bracelets over, and 'she may have genius and many good qualities but, you know, it is impossible to look for them under those mittens'. At Kurnaul, a scattered cantonment, 'all barracks and dust and guns and soldiers', the ladies were dreadfully *démodées* and one Mrs V . . . 'appeared in a turban made, I think, of stamped tin moulded into two fans from which descended a long *pleureuse* feather floating over some very full sleeves'.

Not only were the ladies ill-dressed, ill-bred or both, Emily observed, but they invariably came in the wrong quantities. Relatively few women ventured to India in the first half of the nineteenth century and those who did were frequently 'in an interesting condition' or staying at the hill-stations. At regimental balls therefore there might be but six dancing ladies for every twenty-five men, so that the couples had to dance first on one side, then on the other in the quadrilles until the fair few were quite exhausted. It was an artificial situation for both sexes that resulted in a number of hasty and ill-considered marriages, as Emily noted, describing two Misses D., recently arrived to join a married sister. A 'knowing-looking' pair apparently, appropriately equipped with the most fashionable gowns and head-dresses. 'They are the only young ladies at the station, so I suppose will have their choice of the three regiments; but it is a bad business when all is done. They arrived just in time for this gay week, which will give the poor girls a very false impression of the usual tenor of their lives.'

For the Eden sisters, elevated by their rank above situations of this sort, life retained its hectic tenor, relieved by the first visit to Simla in the summer of 1838 – the one place in India, Emily said, which really was worth all the trouble of getting there. But come autumn, they were again doomed to the road, for a ceremonial state visit to the ruler of the Punjab, Ranjit Singh, at the town of Ferozepore in Ludhiana. The object of this visit was to ratify the terms of a new Sikh–British alliance which Macnaghten and other advisers had been negotiating during the summer. The earlier treaty between the two nations had been made in 1809, soon after the 'Lion of Lahore' came to power. He ruled with masterful ferocity, his greatest strength the well-disciplined and efficient Sikh army which he used to increase his territories by conquest – including the capture of Peshawar across the River Indus that had formerly belonged to the Afghans.

Afghanistan, that was what it was all about – a cunning, virile, poverty-stricken, cynical country which refused to accept its obvious geographical role as reliable buffer-state between the

Middle East and British India. In 1838 the Amir of Afghanistan was Dost Mahomed, an enterprising warrior of ambiguous allegiances who had battled to the top after a turbulent series of tribal plots, fights and counter-plots that followed the defeat of the former ruler, Shah Soojah. Early in the century Soojah had signed a treaty of friendship with the British – which stated that the two countries 'shall in no manner interfere in each other's countries' – and after his deposition the Shah had been in exile in Ludhiana under British protection.

When Lord Auckland went to India he was burdened with a secret directive from the East India Company's committee of directors that the slippery state of Afghan affairs was to be looked into 'either to prevent an extension of Persian dominion in that quarter or to raise a timely barrier against the imperial encroachment of Russian influence'. Once settled in Calcutta, Auckland was further burdened with a great quantity of conflicting advice from his government members on the trustworthiness of Dost Mahomed, the actual intentions of the Persians and Russians with regard to the north-west frontier and the true feelings of the Afghans themselves. Ignoring the last, Auckland made the most disastrous decision of his political career: that the most effective way to forestall Russian encroachment and secure the stability of Afghanistan was to restore the elderly but still aspiring Shah Soojah to the throne of Kabul, and to do this by sending a military expedition made up of levies raised by the Shah, supported by British and Sikh forces.

After reaching that decision in the cool hills during the summer, G. issued a 'Declaration on the Part of the Right Honorable Governor-General of India' that became known as the Simla Manifesto, which set out his justification for the proposed invasion of Afghanistan. It was an erroneous, distorted and hypocritical document ('the welfare and happiness of the Afghans' was, of course, the prime British objective), and it was severely criticized by all in London and Calcutta who had a true grasp of Afghan affairs. But Auckland was determined and, as his elder sister who knew him better than anyone else explained, it was impossible 'to get out of his Lordship's head what had once been put into it'.

So that was why, in early November, it was away from Simla and back to the tents – which had been patched and repaired, reminding Emily only too vividly of the muddy trials and windy tatters of yesteryear. Indeed there were no improvements, and the march began again 'just as it left off'. The cavalcade was rather less cumbrous because 'all the women and other superfluous baggage' had to be left behind, which meant that Mary Wimberley, again pregnant, stayed in the hills. The only essential females were considered to be the Eden sisters and Mrs Macnaghten, which made the whole camp atmosphere more 'melancholy'. Emily had acquired a beautiful new Arab though who 'threw out his legs as if he were going to pick up a pin at a great distance' and some lovely bonnets that arrived just before she left the hills. Although packed a year before, they emerged from the box 'as fresh as if the milliner's girl had just stepped over with them from the shop on the corner'. Emily determined to save the finest one for Ferozepore, 'to give Ranjit Singh some slight idea of what's what in the matter of bonnets'.

What, if anything, Ranjit thought of Miss Eden's bonnets is not on record; what she thought of him, when she first sat at his side on a gold sofa, is. 'Exactly like an old mouse, with grey whiskers and one eye ... no jewels on whatever, nothing but the commonest red silk dress. He had two stockings on at first, which was considered an unusual circumstance; but he very soon contrived to slip one off, that he might sit with one foot in his hand, comfortably'. She wrote that on 29th November, the day after the first official encounter between the Sikhs and British who had spread their great camps over the plains on either side of the River Sutlej near Ferozepore.

During the meeting there was the customary ceremonial exchange of presents, but on a particularly lavish scale. From Ranjit, Emily most admired 'a bed with gold legs, completely encrusted with rubies and emeralds'; from the British, Ranjit crowed with delight over seven horses, two howitzers ornamented with the Punjabi Star and his own profile, and a portrait of Queen Victoria that Emily had painted specially for him. She had reproduced the regal image from prints and descriptions of the

31

coronation robes and the picture was framed in gold set with turquoise and enamelled with the orders of the Garter and the Bath. 'In short it will be puffect, entirely puffect,' she told a friend, 'but I think they ought to give me Ranjit's return present, as it has cost me much trouble to invent a whole Queen, robes and all.' In practice, all presents received were immediately whisked away by the aides-de-camp and stored in treasure chests, some for later distribution to other rajahs, for it was an inflexible rule that none of the Company's servants should receive and keep gifts from natives.

That initial meeting signalled the beginning of two weeks of frenetic ceremonial activity, with fireworks and balls, suppers and dancing girls, and military parades for each force to show the other how fine it was, all accompanied by salutes from Ranjit's personalized howitzers. Even the more sombre rituals of the church went splendidly and Wimberley gave a number of sermons so stirring that Ranjit sent for him to explain why the English congregated in such numbers every Sunday. Wimberley went, armed with translations of the Lord's Prayer and the Ten Commandments, which Emily thought, 'must have been a puzzle – from not worshipping graven images down to not coveting his neighbour's goods'. For the Lion of Lahore had done a lot of successful neighbourly-goods coveting in his time – after a promising start twenty years before, when he had wheedled the famous Koh-i-noor diamond out of Shah Soojah under false pretences. His love of a large glitter was still apparent in the heavily bejewelled costumes of his Sikh followers, three or four of whom together looked 'like Astley's broke loose', Emily commented.

At last, when everyone of any consequence was utterly surfeited with food, drink and splendour and Emily had seen so many emeralds, pearls and diamonds that she had quite lost any wish to possess them, the leaders of the two armies swore eternal friendship to each other and the camps were struck. For the Edens, it was a move towards another state occasion at Lahore, the Sikh capital; for the men of the Bengal Army it was a move towards the north-west frontier and the unknown perils of Afghanistan; for Charles Wimberley, it was a sudden urgent call back to Simla 'for his wife's *accouchement*. He will go scrambling up to Simla in a shorter time than the post goes,' Emily forecast. 'He borrows a horse here and rides a camel there and the Putteealah Rajah is to lend him a palanquin, and he set off with some cold dinner in one hand and Culpepper's Midwifery in the other, which he borrowed off Doctor Drummond at the last minute.'

An appropriate last picture of Charles, frantically just-coping as usual, and, as usual, a source of quiet amusement for his superiors. Mary, who kept no more diaries, was safely delivered of a daughter, Julia, and the Wimberleys stayed in India for the remainder of Auckland's term of office. When they left they had been seventeen years in the East and had survived their fair share of illness and trouble. Happily, they both lived to celebrate their golden wedding in pastoral Kent and tell stories to their grand-children of the Governor-General's Grand Processional across India.

Chapter Three

That stagey encounter between the British and Sikhs in the winter of 1838 was an apogee of the traditional form of tributary and diplomatic exchange between East and West. As a later historian puts it: 'In high quarters where Governor-Generals had to deal with equal or only just inferior native powers, it was a question of glorious pageants and assemblies; all the circumstances which outsiders mistake for the essential East; presents and counter-presents, until Lord Auckland and Ranjit Singh . . . began to assume some of the glory of Henry VIII and Francis I on the Field of the Cloth of Gold.'

More medieval than modern, in short, and many of the younger civilian and military officers around at the time distrusted these transitory, ceremonial meetings; they were beginning to ask themselves how relationships between the two countries would develop, and were prepared to devote their lives to the influencing and strengthening of the British Empire in India – in the light of their own principles. They were zealous men with a deep sense of Christian duty, a sympathetic commitment to the Indians as people, and proven abilities as soldierly administrators. Foremost among them was Henry Lawrence, later typecast as a classic hero of Victoria's India, but, in late 1838, merely one of the hundreds of newly arrived personnel placed at the disposal of their Commanders-in-Chief, ready for active service in the field if required and meanwhile marching and mooching about on the plains near Ferozepore in Lord Auckland's unwieldy camp.

As a senior lieutenant in the Bengal Artillery, Lawrence was on the Edens' invitee list and describes his first meeting with them.

'Currie [his friend] and I strolled about camp and saw the two ornamental howitzers that are to be presented to Ranjit Singh. We also saw Lord Auckland and Miss Eden (junior) sitting in front of their tent, and a band of music on four elephants practising . . . I had an invitation to dinner: at half-past six I went prepared to scrutinize her [i.e. Emily Eden] who is said to resemble my love, and so far she does that she has a long fair face, but she is loud and vulgar and talks only rot. Lord Auckland is a quiet, frostbitten chap . . . I sat beside him at dinner and his conversation was soon exhausted, though not his appetite.' In the matter of ladies, Henry Lawrence was undoubtedly biased, for he was but recently married to his love and was brimful of the passion for her that had been pent up in him for the previous nine years.

Her name was Honoria, they were cousins and met in 1827 through family connections when he was home on sick leave after experiencing his first taste of India as a subaltern in the Bengal Artillery. The disciplined rigours of that life had developed his deeply implanted sense of duty towards his family and his work, so, although he had wanted to marry Honoria then, he returned to India in 1829 'without speaking' of the matter. Honoria was left – as many a serious-minded young woman of her time – with little hope of marrying the man she loved, no desire to marry anyone else, and scant resources or encouragement to fill her days instead with any of the meaningful activities open to young men. She felt, she wrote later, as if 'the unemployed energies, the unsatisfied desire for usefulness would eat me up'; she became engaged and broke it off; she worked as a governess for two years, resigned, but not satisfied, with her lot. The two cousins maintained a link of communication through Letitia Lawrence, Henry's favourite sister and Honoria's close friend, and at last, in 1836, with Letitia as a devoted go-between suggesting what neither of them dare express, Henry wrote to Honoria asking if she would go out to India and marry him. She accepted, of course, as eagerly and ardently as the girl he had left behind would have done, confident that, during seven years of separation, their mutual recognition had not atrophied.

She left England in April 1837, confessing that she had always felt 'miserably half-ish' without him. 'We are both constituted more than most people to find all we want in each other,' she told him. To an extent this was true; but it was more true for her, because he had also dedicated himself to India with a fervour of ambitious, high-minded purpose that devoured most of his time and energy. But this very dynamism attracted her to him; she accepted his causes as her own, but did so without losing the integrity of her own personality.

The first months of their married life were idyllic. Henry was a revenue surveyor in the north-west and had to travel long distances mapping villages, assessing the quantity and quality of arable land, counting heads, establishing boundaries. It gave him that rice-roots experience of peasant India which became, for him and other British administrators, the touchstone of their future policies. And Honoria gained this too, because she went with him. She enjoyed every hour of it, though, compared to the leisurely luxury of camp-life Auckland-style, the going was tough. 'One who minds living on mutton and fowls for six months in the year had better not marry a surveyor,' she wrote home. 'Our life in camp teaches us how many "indispensables" we can do without.'

In any case, she had all she really wanted – the stimulus of foreign travel, freedom from what she termed the 'superfluities of society' and the love of one who was 'so thoroughly a companion'. 'I am sitting in our wee hill-tent, our chattels all packed except for two chairs, a gun case . . . and the fireplace – a delightful bit of furniture, the grate set on legs with a stove-like chimney . . . In some marshy ground close by, the elephant and his mahout are amusing themselves, and under the straw mat set on four sticks, the servants are preparing breakfast, smoking hookahs, packing up.' One of Henry's assistants, Lieutenant Abbott, long remembered seeing them thus together, in a rough region of the Nepal foothills where fires had to be kept alight to ward off tigers. He wrote, 'When we met, to my surprise I found Mrs Lawrence with her husband. She was seated on the bank of a nullah her feet overhanging the den of some wild animal, while she, with a portfolio in her lap, was writing overland letters and her husband, at no great distance, was laying his theodolite.' As Abbott got to know her, he decided she was 'one in a thousand – highly gifted in mind, of a most cheerful disposition'. They were at one in all they did, 'she and he both in their glory'.

But the very intensity of their love held the seeds of future separations. By early 1838 she was pregnant, decidedly a mixed blessing for her. 'I rejoice with trembling at the prospect,' she confessed, realizing that she could no longer be her husband's constant companion. 'If I had the choice I could not venture to decide on such a gift – but that is appointed by a Power beyond our own.' This was written in the journal which she and Henry shared and in which they expressed their thoughts to each other through a written conversation that was their way round the emotional inhibitions of the time. It was a quaint device but it helped them to bridge their long periods of separation and has left posterity with an unusually intimate glimpse into the personal lives of a Victorian hero and his mate.

As her pregnancy advanced, Honoria found that she had to follow after Henry on his journeys in a hated dhoolie as if she were another 'item of baggage', instead of riding freely at his side. But she stuck it as long as she could. As the temperature rose, they fashioned an 'underground tent' for her, in which, hopefully, she could escape the worst of the heat. It was a large hole, four feet deep, dug in the shade of trees and surrounded by high earth walls above ground, with two openings screened by woven grass. Its interior gloom was only 80 degrees compared to the harsh 95 outside, but dust and dead mango leaves whirled in the hot wind through its openings, the screens flapped; there was nothing to do there but wait for the relief of sunset and Henry's return from his surveying.

Eventually she gave up and settled down in a house, where she began fully to realize the restrictions of the life she had chosen. For women in India there could be 'no delightful rambling walks, no visiting the poor, no going out alone unquestioned'. (Even for one of Honoria's wide sympathy there were apparently no visitable 'poor' in India.) Confined to an ordinary military station she was at the mercy of the 'social superfluities' she always disliked. Among the women there was little discussion of public topics and one heard the same trivia 'with far more monotony than in one of our provincial towns'. During many a dinner-party, the stuffiness of the room and sheer quantity of the food made her fall nearly asleep, the only sight pleasing to her drowsy eye being the symmetrical arrangement of dark and light – the men's dress entirely white and, behind the guests, 'a complete circle of dark faces and white turbans; each servant behind his master's chair'. There was a routine deadliness about the life that appalled her, for she had wrested a certain freedom from conventionality and was married to a highly original man. Here, for the most part, the married couples 'went out for their evening drive on the same dusty road where they had driven a thousand times, meeting the same faces they have met a hundred times. When they come in there is dinner; then coffee; then bed. So passes day after day till the corps or the civilian is removed; and they settle down else-where to plod on the same eternal round.'

The last months of her pregnancy were weighted with sickness, a 'strange deadness of the spirit' and the tormenting presentiment that she would die in childbirth. In a moving 'secret letter' on the theme she wrote to Henry, 'I would lay down my life for you. And if I am not to survive, I shall feel it is for your good to be left alone.' But the immediate threat of parting was of another kind, for by that time the news of the coming Afghan campaign was abroad and Henry, in spite of his wife's condition, applied at once to return to active duty. It was her first experience of the fact that duty and ambition overruled his life; even she had to take second place. In the event he did not leave immediately, she did not die, and on 6th September when their son Alexander was born, Henry wrote in their journal, 'I stayed with you my darling at your wish. But the sight of your suffering is scarcely re-paid even by our Boy.'

Just three weeks after the birth his recall came and they left together on the long overland journey to Cawnpore, Honoria and the baby travelling by dhoolie behind Henry on horseback. It was not an easy introduction to life for Alec and he was incessantly sick from her milk. In the middle of one particularly wretched night she got out of the jolting vehicle on to the dark and desolate plain and 'carried my babe about till I almost fainted. At last I laid him on my cloak by the roadside; but he cried so fearfully that I picked him up again. I thought he would die there and then; and I so worn and weak that I had no self-control to sustain me.' At length Henry rode back to find out what was wrong. He bought some goat's milk for the baby and then urged them onwards. By the time they reached Cawnpore she was so ill she had to stay behind while he pushed on alone towards the north-west. But she did not stay for long. At sunset on 18th December she set off again in one palki, 'the babe and nurse in the other and sixteen black men, eight to each palki, and two men with a roll of flax and rags made into a torch which they feed from a skin bottle of oil as they run'. They ran continuously, through head-high corn, filthy town streets, unmarked empty plains until, she later recorded, 'On January 1st 1839 I entered the camp of the Army of the Indus at Ferozepore'.

. . . 'There! We left Lahore yesterday, we have made two marches and shall cross the river in four more.' wrote Emily Eden on New Year's Day, 1839. As Ferozepore was about forty miles from Lahore and very close to the Sutlej River in question, the two fair ladies of somewhat similar aspect just missed meeting on that occasion – which did not grieve either of them. For Honoria wanted only to see Henry, and Emily was concerned mainly about the crossing of all the inconvenient rivers that lay between her and the eventual haven of Simla. They managed the Sutlej well enough, but then came to a 'wretched little rivulet' called the Gugga, in the district of Hansi, which chose to rise beyond all reasonable and expected proportions on 24th January, just as they reached it. So they all had to sit down along the banks and wait for it to subside. The gentlemen went shooting and 'G.' killed ten quails and an antelope, which was considered quite a feat; the ladies stayed in their tents, fuming at the nonchalance of 'Mr N.', the magistrate on the opposite bank, 'who ought to be wringing his hands constantly and plying eternally between our camp and the river, a victim to remorse that he had not made a bridge of boats in time; instead of which N.'s tents are seen in the distance on the other side of the river and he never stirs from them, and all the notice he has taken of us is a message that perhaps he had better go back and prepare for us at Hansi as there seems little chance of our crossing for a week.'

Actually, and inconceivably to Emily, 'N.', whose real name was Samuel Sneade Brown, was enormously relieved at the behaviour of the Gugga and only wished it would continue indefinitely in full unfordable spate. For Brown was a man of retiring habits and embittered by eleven lonely humdrum years in the Company's service as a magistrate and collector. He was not old, but he felt it; he was not really unsociable but circumstances had made him so. 'I long for something to amuse me during the intervals of business and study,' he wrote home to his mother soon after his arrival in India. '. . . Some source of interest, friendship or affection; there is a void which I would were filled.' Yet he was not convinced that the average English memsahib could fill it, mainly because the native women 'were so amusingly playful, so anxious to please that a person, after being accustomed to their society, shrinks from the idea of encountering the whims or yielding to the furies of an Englishwoman . . . As for myself,' he declared, 'I feel certain that I shall never marry in this country; and I shall be so ugly and so yellow after ten years of residence here that no one but broken-down old maids would have me.'

And so, still unmarried, shy, set in his lonesome ways and unused to sophisticated after-dinner chat, Brown was appalled to learn that Lord Auckland with his sisters – whom he probably regarded as broken-down old maids – were coming his way, 'merely to while away the time until the season comes for retiring to the hills'. The day before their arrival he would have to ride eighteen miles to their camp, he wrote in his journal, and he would have to wait upon his Lordship and the Chief Secretary and call upon the Misses Eden. 'I wish them all at the bottom of the sea, and my wish will, I doubt not, be in part fulfilled, as the Gugga River which is the boundary of my domains has been much swollen by late rains and there is only one ferry boat and that a small one, so that if they escape a ducking personally their traps will get a beautiful wetting.' So no wonder he had not bestirred himself to build a bridge of boats, as Emily thought he should, and that he continued to watch developments from a complacent distance. 'Some of the baggage has crossed,' he wrote the next day, 'and cannot now get back again, so that the camp is in a pretty mess; all of which I enjoy extremely. I am fairly sick of this work and as cross as a bear with a sore head.'

That the fording, when it eventually took place, was a spectacle worth the waiting for, both Brown and Emily, from their different vantage points, agreed. Brown wrote, 'I never saw such a scene of confusion. The noise and row were beyond everything.' 'I never saw such a scene as the ghaut,' Emily wrote. 'Such a conglomeration of carts, sepoys, bullocks, trunks etc, and six hundred camels who would not go any way.' The English in charge of the boats each had on 'their broad white feather hats to keep off the sun and a long stick to keep the people from crowding – and looked like pictures of slave drivers and were screaming and gesticulating and hauling packages in and out.' The camels were forced across by tying them in strings of six to the tail of an elephant who swam over tugging them behind. Some of the hackeries disappeared under water altogether; bullocks plunged about, their drivers hanging to their tails; the coachman's pet bear was almost drowned.

The Governor and his ladies crossed without mishap however and, noted Emily, 'that villain N . . . met us at the ghaut – not the least ashamed of himself'. 'I was waiting on the bank to receive them,' says Brown, 'and paid my respects to his Lordship and a visit to the Misses Eden in the course of the day . . . In the evening I dined with them, and every day as long as I remain with the camp. It is very stiff and starch-neck-clothed sort of work; but having no decent excuse I cannot shrink.'

And he put up a good front apparently. 'By no means an unpolished *jungle*-man,' Emily decided of him (that being the term for those poor whites who had been totally isolated for so long in the various Indian wildernesses that their civilized manners and small-talk had been quite 'jungled' out of them). But Brown was 'rather the contrary, jolly and pleasant, only that he has nearly forgotten his English. He laughs like that Dr G. . . . we used to know and says with a great ho-ho-ho, "If it hadn't been for the inconvenience on account of supplies, it is just as well you should have been stopped in this way. You would to see the hard*ships* of camp life." I wonder what the ships of a camp are which are not *hard*ships?' And actually, though the Edens were obviously a bunch of pampered aristocrats, he did not find them quite so over-bearing and snooty as he had feared. 'Clever and sensible women' those two spinster sisters and 'his Lordship seems a good sort of man, but nothing striking, either in manner or appearance'. Nevertheless they hung about far too long '. . . deuce take them all. The trouble they give is quite inconceivable and no thanks for it either. This is the way with great people.'

So at length the 'great people' trundled on towards the promise of a Simla spring, leaving the minor characters to clear up the mess they left behind – the ladies to stow away their best ball-gowns in tin-lined trunks, the gentlemen to ponder how good an impres-sion they had made upon the inscrutable Lord A. But a few, like the Lawrences, great people of a very different sort, bothered little about ball-gowns and good impressions; there was far too much to be done.

Certainly this was the case at Ferozepore, a neglected little town that had suddenly gained significance as a military and political post because it was near the Punjab and on the direct route from Delhi to the Afghan frontier. Just after Henry Lawrence had arrived there, that ill-fated division of the Bengal Army, called the Army of the Indus – made up of about 9,500 English troops, 6,000 men raised by Shah Soojah, the whole severely hampered by no less than 38,000 camp-followers – started off on the British expedition to Afghanistan. The other military division (to which Henry was assigned) stayed in India as an 'Army of Observation'. Chagrined at his exclusion from active duty after all, Henry agi-tated for work more excitingly political than surveying, and, early in 1839, he was given civil charge of Ferozepore as 'Assistant to the Governor-General's Agent for the Affairs of the Punjab and the North-West frontier'. The job entailed acting as town-planner, civil engineer, transport officer, magistrate and post-master for the entire district and he threw all his dynamic energy into it.

Ferozepore then was a sprawling collection of rough wooden huts, a few dingy shops and alleyways 'crammed to the throat with dogs, filth and old women', Honoria wrote. Seen from the surrounding plain – 'a wilderness of cacti, prickly scrub, sandy hillocks and the bleached bones of camels and bullocks' – the town's only salient feature was a dilapidated mud-and-brick fort perched on a hill; in two of its rooms, windowless 'little pigeon-holes' with an open floor-gap between them, and ramshackle doors through which the dust blew incessantly, Honoria and her baby were installed.

But as long as she was with her husband the discomforts did not in the least trouble her, and she now brought to motherhood the same spirit of earnest endeavour that she had taken to India and to Henry himself. Her journal, she resolved, would be a record of 'the treatment I give Alec's body and mind, and I will strive impartially to note each trial and its result. Moreover to mark down faithfully such faults as I find in myself and think most likely to injure my infant.' And there – in now-faded sepia on coarse, brownish journal-paper – is an account of her baby's troubled early days in cheerless Ferozepore Fort. He had a cough; she gave him a mixture of gum arabic, vinegar, sugar and peche-chuan wine; he had various kinds of irregular motions, so she dosed him with castor oil, Gregory's powder and aniseed; he had ophthalmia caused by the gritty winds and she pounded unguents for his eyes. But in spite of her efforts he continued to ail and 'the intense anxiety I feel about my treasure is a great alloy to the happiness of having him'. So there was another divisive tug for her always-strained nerves – she longed only to be with Henry wherever he was, but his work was on the searing hot or freezing plains, and her child needed the healthy air of the hills. So, in mid-March, conforming more reluctantly than most to the customs of the mothering memsahibs, she left with Alec for Simla.

Once ensconced in cool and comfortable surroundings she devoted herself to the problems of actually rearing children in India. Coming late to motherhood by the standards of the time, she was critically aware of the hazards of this alien environment on the very young, who were threatened not only by disease and the rigours of the climate, but also by the debilitating effects of being in the continuous and too-reverential care of native servants. She took two offspring of a friend with her to Simla and 'they have the odious whine of all spoilt children,' she wrote. 'They learn nothing but Hindustani ... Till I brought little Susy up here – aged two – I did not know what helpless mortals Anglo-Indian children are; fed, dressed, lifted up and down as if they were dolls. Jemmie, at three and a half, is a healthy, intelligent boy – simply *animalised*. No ideas except to eat and drink and tell lies, fight and tyrannise.' She was horrified to hear the servants calling her own tiny infant 'Lord and Protector of the Poor' and telling him, 'Certainly when you are a man you will flog the black people and please yourself.'

... Which numbers of Alec's generation certainly did; but not, surely, Alexander Lawrence, whose mother, when he was but six months old, made lists of the particularly important virtues which she must inculcate in him: Regularity, Obedience, Independence, Courage, Precision, Industry and Delicacy. The last quality was one that Anglo-Indian children were 'dreadfully deficient in'. 'After he is a year old I mean never to bathe him quite naked,' she decided. Lying on her sofa in the quiet Simla afternoons, she read *Home Education* most thoroughly and found it 'rich in principles to be carried out in practice'. Her earnestness must have irritated some more light-hearted young mothers who apparently wondered aloud how Indian children managed to grow up satisfactorily without quite so much fuss. Yes but then, Honoria would retort, 'they are not called on for strenuous mental exertion, and if we train our children to that we must fortify the body accordingly.'

Had Honoria always lived up to her high-minded ideals for future empire-builders, she would have been insufferable, but, endearingly, both she and Henry were also impulsive, generous and muddle-prone and every new year they made orderly time-schedules that collapsed into disorder before the Spring. 'My time is sadly mis-managed and frittered away,' she confessed. 'One thing to try for is a more legible hand. I often find it difficult to read my own writing.' (Later readers of her journal still wish she had kept to *that* resolution at least.) What she would not do, because her natural cast of mind and her principles were both against it, would be to 'fritter away' her days on Simla's normal social round – to which the Governor-General's sisters were bound, whether they would or no.

Emily and Fanny arrived in Simla that year about the same time as Honoria, very relieved to be out from under canvas. There was something permanent and unchanging about Simla, the nearest place to dear Home that one could hope for in this dreadful country. Most of the British felt like that about it, and had done so long before the Edens arrived. The first European houses were built there in the 1820s and within a decade it had become 'a resort of the rich, idle and invalid', according to a French traveller. The climate was the greatest attraction. One Captain Mundy, writing in 1828, explained that 'the salubrity of this little abode of Hygeia is well attested by the presence of no less than sixteen ladies who gladly embrace the inconveniences attendant upon narrow accommodations and want of equipages for the advantages accruing from the climate to themselves and their children.' Emily put it more pungently: 'Like meat, we keep better here.'

The ladies did not long have to embrace such narrow accommodations for, during the 1830s, a number of sizable houses were built. They were mostly of slate and stone, with real chimneys and cosy names like Woodbine Cottage, The Hermitage, Rookwood, Sunny Bank. Lord William Bentinck, Auckland's predecessor, erected his own Bentinck Castle, and his wife purchased the local billiard room and converted it into Simla's first place of regular Christian worship.

The Edens chose to reside in Auckland House on a north-eastern spur designated 'Elysium' as 'a delicate compliment to the honorable Misses Eden' according to local records. It was not totally idyllic, for it was soon reported that Lord Auckland 'is said to be dissatisfied with his house, and for good reason. It is frittered away in paltry closets six and seven feet square and has only two rooms deserving the name.' And worse yet, the house was one-storied with a flat roof of beaten-down earth which, during the rains, became a seeping mire. According to a local journalist, two of Auckland's staff 'dined every day with umbrellas held over their heads and their dinners'. But Emily thought it was a 'jewel of a little house' for it had real carpets and walls that did not flap in every wind. To make up for the lack of cornices, she cut out paper patterns and had them painted in borders all round the doors and windows. And, looking from the windows, one could see deep valleys, snowy ranges and masses of wild red rhododendron trees. Tulips and lilies bloomed in their season and real birds sang – blackbirds and even cuckoos, though they could not get beyond the 'cuck'.

It was all so delightful and home-like that space was still at a premium and house-rents quite extortionate. The station 'has never been so crowded', reported the East India Magazine. 'Public offices are being converted into private residences and the public bazaar contains a portion of those unable to find accommodation elsewhere.' Finding it difficult to house his numerous staff, George Auckland bought the house adjoining his own and called it 'Secretarys' Lodge'. In its grounds, 'we have found a beautiful terrace for the band,' Emily enthused, 'and we have persuaded P. . . . who is laying out the grounds, to arrange a few pretty paths for two, and also to make the gates so narrow that jonpauns cannot come through them, so that the ladies must be handed out and walk up to the music.'

The proportion of ladies to gentlemen was as unbalanced in the hill-stations as on the plains, and even more annoying. 'There are forty-six ladies and twelve gentlemen in Simla independent of our party,' she noted soon after arrival, 'and forty more ladies and six gentlemen are expected up shortly. How any dancing is to be managed at our parties I cannot make out. The aides-de-camp are in despair about it.' Emily evidently had a soft spot for good-looking aides-de-camp. One set of them, she wrote, 'were so *larking*'. Others were inclined to droop in romantic melancholy. 'Thank goodness,' she wrote of one such set, 'now they are all engaged except L. . . ., who is not likely to fall in love with anybody but himself.' But, larking or love-lorn, they were all most attentive to her needs and so rather pleasant to have around. Much depended, of course, on your viewpoint. An anonymous author of some caustic 'Observations of India' noted, 'Lord Auckland arrived at Simla in company with two elderly maiden ladies, his sisters. Handsome aides-de-camp were here, there and everywhere, and if plains people did not know what the duties of aides-de-camp were, and why so many of them were paid by the State, they might here learn that their employment was to follow these ladies and make themselves generally useful as upper foot-men. What swarms of idleness in mountebank finery does the shade of Monarchy collect around it! Pious youths were not particularly in request in Lord Auckland's house, but good-looking ones held the same premium as with his predecessor.'

The worries of the aides-de-camp were somewhat lessened by the numbers of ladies who chose to remain 'retired' from the social round owing to their husbands' absence on active duty – 'very devoted wives,' Emily remarked acidly, 'but if the war lasts they will be very dull women.' However even they could usually be persuaded to come along to the terrace at Secretarys' Lodge, look at the spectacular views over the distant Snowy Range and 'console themselves with a little music and take a little tea and coffee and talk a little'. And perhaps Honoria Lawrence was among them: though she was probably labelled by Emily as one of the dull, she did sometimes visit Auckland House, where the hours were sensibly early and the talk was of a higher order than at most tables where, she admitted, 'I either sit silent and look grumpy or join in what I hate and condemn.' Those who attended balls had in turn to give them, and the 'expense of this in a poor country, the dislocation of family arrangements and the scandals and jealousies that follow are all at variance with sound Christian thinking'. For ladies to withdraw themselves for these principles was valid in the Edens' eyes, though they did not concur; but to do so simply because their husbands were at war was really rather foolish – especially when, with regard to Afghanistan, there was no cause whatever for alarm.

In May there came the most cheering dispatches from Envoy Macnaghten to say that the Army of the Indus had marched into the city of Candahar without opposition and that the natives seemed delighted to welcome Shah Soojah as their new ruler and let Dost Mahomed flee into the wilderness. It was such a heartening vindication of G.'s judgement, Emily felt. All Simla celebrated and the wives who were earlier forlorn now 'see with their minds' eye their husbands eating apricots and drinking acid sherbert and they are satisfied'.

Opportunely, the arrival of the news coincided with the Ball in honour of the Queen's birthday which was held at Annandale, a pleasantly proportioned valley of shaded fir and pine groves and already renowned as Simla's public playground. A 'romantic glen', a 'picturesque dell' where couples, not always married, could discreetly dally. *Fêtes champêtres*, fancy fairs and riding parties were all the rage there and, the previous year, the Eden sisters had helped to organize one of its largest ever fairs – ten pavilions aflap with coloured bunting, a luncheon marquee and a vast array of 'pretty commodities – all that silk, satin, lace and embroidery with their manifold concomitants could produce laid out in elegant style, on sale for charitable good works,' wrote a gentleman visitor.

But his eye was less fastidious than Honoria's who felt that these 'fancy goods' were 'of the most useless kind and the manufacture and purchase of them fosters the love of these frivolities . . . Besides, the odious bad taste of most of the articles disgusts me.' Moreover, competition over the production of these 'odious articles' brought out the worst in some women. Would-be artists discussed each other's work with malice, and, reported Honoria, 'I said to Mrs Codrington, "I think the work of Mrs L. . . . a former governess shews more knowledge of the art than any of the rest." She replied sneeringly, "Oh of course it must do . . . It was her trade to teach."' And that, feared Honoria who had also once been in the teaching trade, was a fair sample of Simla-style conversation, which was no more than 'a confused bundle of tinsel, rags and dirt, the contents of a dust-pan; a many-sided buzz of scandal and vanity, hasty censure, mutilated praise and insincere professions'. Simla also had the unenviable reputation of being more racially prejudiced than most parts of the Company's India. The year before, when the Sikh envoys from Ranjit Singh had stayed there for preliminary talks on the future British–Sikh treaty, Simla's ladies had at first announced they would not attend the ball in their honour because they 'had no idea of dancing before natives'. Utter nonsense, Emily continued. 'Considering we ask forty natives to every dance we give in Calcutta and nobody ever cares.' All the invited ladies but three eventually came, and so did the Sikhs, who were 'very quiet and well-behaved'. Two of them had seen English-style dancing before and were well aware that the ladies were not nautch-girls. Emily hoped 'they explained that very important fact to the others'.

An advantage of being at the top of the topmost tree was that one could set the tone on matters like this and avoid much of the 'dirt and tinsel' below – one had only to preside at the polished end-production. At that Annandale ball, for instance, which in Emily's view turned out a most triumphal dual celebration of the young monarch's birthday and the news from Afghanistan: champagne toasts, fireworks, dancing on a platform arched with flowers, and, among the trees, the words Victoria and Candahar emblazoned in letters twelve foot high.

A nearby Hindu temple was also asparkle with lanterns and streamers, and 'Vishnu or Mahadevi to whom I believe it really belonged must have been affronted', Emily thought, withdrawing herself a little and realizing how incongruous and knife-edge it all was. 'Twenty years ago no European had ever been here, and there we were, with the band playing the *Puritani* and *Masaniello* and eating salmon from Scotland and sardines from the Mediterranean, and observing that St Cloup's *potage à la Julienne* was perhaps better than his other soups, and that some of the ladies' sleeves were too tight according to the overland fashions for March etc.; and all this in the face of those high hills, some of which have remained untrodden since the creation, and we hundred and five Europeans being surrounded by at least 3,000 mountaineers, who, wrapped up in their hill-blankets, looked on at what we call our polite amusements, and bowed to the ground if a European came near them. I sometimes wonder they do not cut all our heads off and say nothing more about it.'

This sudden, vividly expressed, uneasy awareness of the dark watching country through which the British so confidently trampled and pranced was unusual for Emily Eden, who retained her equilibrium by accepting the conventional limitations of her position and operating cleverly within them. But for others, a minority, India itself, pulsating and incalculable, was always the touchstone of reality and places like Simla no more than airy-fairy refuges to which one retreated only to regain health and strength. Such a one was Honoria Lawrence, and, as soon as autumn came, she took up her now restored infant and went hurrying gladly back to Henry and the veritable life of men and events on the plains below.

It was a time of great activity in Ferozepore. Ranjit Singh had died the previous summer and, for the next five years, the Sikh kingdom was disrupted by factions fighting for the military supremacy that only he had been able to maintain single-handed. The disruption worried the British, who could no longer count on the goodwill of the powerful Sikh army or the certainty of peace on the Sikh–Indian frontier. Of more immediate moment was the fact that the Army of the Indus, after waiting around at Candahar for two months, had moved on to Kabul, captured it on 6th August and reinstated Shah Soojah on the throne.

It became clear even to the myopic leaders of the British forces that, once arrived in the capital, they could not simply go away again and leave Soojah to rule – he had to be propped up with military backing, and indefinitely. So, in due course, part of the Army of the Indus became an army of occupation, quartered first in the old citadel of Balla Hissar which dominated Kabul, and later in purpose-built cantonments situated a mile to the north-east on low swampy ground which did not dominate anything and were very vulnerable to attack from the various overlooking hill forts. The Army's Commissariat bought up what local supplies it could – storing them in a building *outside* the cantonments' perimeter – and arranged for the delivery of other more expensive long-term necessities, such as wives and children, wines and cigars, to be sent through from India.

As Ferozepore was on the main supply route to the border, it thrummed with activity – men and baggage constantly moving through in either direction, camps pitched and struck, workmen arriving to build larger barracks, wives and children jolting through in dhoolies, cavalry officers swishing along regimental lines, hordes of camp-followers sleeping rough. Henry Lawrence worked to full stretch, overwrought with his responsibilities, for, as an officer of the Political Department, he was, as his biographer and fellow-officer Herbert Edwardes says, supposed to provide those passing through with anything – 'a map, a camel, a wet nurse, a spy, a guide-elephant or a sack of grain' – and if supplies failed, he got the blame. Finding that his staff was insufficient to handle the greatly increased volume of mail and dispatches, Henry enlisted his wife's aid. In a letter to his superiors complaining of the ramshackle administrative machinery, he says, 'the treasury and post office have been my worst troubles . . . When I took charge of the post office, letters for all unknown persons in India came here and there were no writers. Mrs Lawrence and I have been six, eight, ten hours in the post office in the day, or rather during the night.'

Harried as they were however, they continued to make hopeful new schedules for orderly joint endeavour. One of Honoria's for this time read: 'Rise at four a.m. Reading and prayer; arrange Henry's papers, copy his letters. Go out with him or read at home.' Then there were two hours for household affairs, two more for the study of Hindustani. Henry had a more demanding time-table for work, exercise, meals – but, on the opposite page, there is a Sunday entry: 'Nothing much today except break all our rules.'

Nor was there much chance for Honoria to relax in the small bungalow they had eventually obtained. She was pregnant again; it was summer again; 'the sun grinning at us through a hot haze'; Alec was fretful, wispy, given to ferocious tantrums that alarmed her. Added to this, the ever-hospitable Henry turned their home into just another staging-post. 'I am thoroughly sick of hospitality,' Honoria complained to him in their joint journal. 'In little more than two months I have had twelve guests staying, two, three or four weeks each; besides many times having folks to dinner . . . The expense is great, but I would gladly pay the money to avoid the trouble. It is so annoying to pass day after day without ever sitting down *tête à tête*, never able to leave my room without finding men lounging in the dining-room or verandah – our nice evenings quite cut up. What pleasant ones, darling, we often had alone, sitting close together at the table, reading, writing, talking, eating – as it might be; all with that exclusive feeling of companionship that is the very sunshine of life.'

But she had married a dynamically ambitious man; he needed to know people, to have first-hand accounts of what was happening on all the troubled frontiers. Much as he loved Honoria's company, he chafed to be in Kabul himself with his brother George, who had been made Personal Assistant to Macnaghten, the British Envoy and 'adviser' of Shah Soojah. Twice Henry requested to be sent there and was refused – refusals that immensely, though secretly, relieved Honoria and filled him with frustration and envy. A lucky fellow, his brother, to be there in Kabul when the Afghans and the British were assumed to be settling down to horse-racing and hunting together in mutual harmony and the leaders of the successful campaign were basking in the shine of honours sent out from England. 'All things considered,' wrote Sir William Macnaghten, newly created a Baronet, to Lord Auckland, newly created an Earl, 'the perfect tranquillity of the country is to my mind perfectly miraculous. Already our presence has been infinitely beneficial in allaying animosities and pointing out abuses.'

Chapter Four

So the British presence in India and neighbouring Afghanistan was being remorselessly consolidated – an 'infinitely beneficial' presence which required the services of men endowed with much purposeful endeavour like Henry Lawrence and much dignity of office like Lord Auckland. And there was an increasing number of supporting roles to fill, not by men of Henry's calibre perhaps, their wives not blessed with Honoria's whole-hearted dedication – just ordinary people most of them, going a long way to do a job of work in a hot country for a long time.

Mr and Mrs Edward Benthall for example, who set sail for Calcutta aboard the East Indiaman *Southampton* in the summer of 1841. Edward was a member of the I.C.S. and had already spent several years in India, so he had more idea of what to expect than his young wife, Clementina, whom he had recently married and who was heavily pregnant with their first child. Coming from the shelter of her father's Buckinghamshire vicarage, Clementina was not, for a start, prepared for the sheer racket of it all. There were people putting up shelves for books in their cabins and hammering their own items of furniture to the floors; added to the din was the baying of eighty-four hounds belonging to an army captain and the protests of sundry other livestock, most of them embarking on their last journey – thirty pigs, two milch cows with calves, forty sheep, flocks of geese, ducks, hens and several cages of singing birds.

The thud and rush of the pumps and the scrubbing of the quarter-deck began with every dawn and, after breakfast, the Pianos began. 'Five Pianos in separate cabins,' Clementina recorded despondently, 'and three frequently used at once, and as each performer played a distinct tune or ran up and down the scales as practice, the blending of harmonious sounds became horrible discord and the ear was even more pained when the instruments were out of tune.' The passengers could also muster a violinist, two guitarists, three horn-players and, worst of all, 'some of the young ladies during a large portion of the day were singing solfeggios at the highest pitch of their voices'.

If Clementina could have joined in she might not have minded, but, what with the vessel's rolling and the advanced state of her pregnancy, food 'seldom remained with me an hour' – even though it was only arrowroot, sago or broth. She was soon too weak to leave her cabin or even brush the flies from her face, and her bones showed through her skin. To cheer her, Edward and the music-loving ladies brought her the latest shipboard gossip: the sailors had caught a shark off Madeira, flying fish had landed on deck in the night, the caged goldfinches had died and so had some of the Calcutta-bound hounds. Clementina felt it was her turn next and 'as my hour of trial drew near I thought death would probably close my long illness.' However, on 28th August after 'a day and night of dreadful suffering' with 'poor Edward' rushing about in distraction, 'I ushered into this world my first son.' The birth was duly noted in the ship's log as having occurred four degrees north of the Equator, and, a few days later, they crossed the line – to celebrate which the sailors 'drank much grog and shot lots of Cape pigeons'.

Although Clementina was at last able to leave her cabin, her ordeals were not yet over, for, after rounding the Cape, they ran into the most fearful storm which 'surprised even the Captain' and lasted a week. As the vessel was buffeted by the waves the baby's swinging cot crashed against the cabin ceiling and Clementina had to tie a handkerchief to one side of her couch, 'by which I kept myself from falling out on the opposite side, whilst with one arm I clasped my little boy'. The next day the waves broke right through the portholes and the cabin floor was awash; in the cuddy, teapots and glasses scudded up and down the tables and smashed, and the night was even more alarming – the masts creaked horribly and, after one searing lightning flash, one of the yards snapped, some of the sails giving way, and the carpenter and sailmaker were almost drowned while making emergency repairs.

Then the weather cleared, the rope- and sailmakers spread the damaged sails out on deck and repaired them at leisure in the sun. One could lean over the rails and watch the fish swimming near the deep blue surface, the drifting purple reflections of the flimsy clouds, the dolphins looping about the horizons. Some of the 'young gentlemen' caught albatrosses with hooks and lines, which they gave to the sailors – who cut off the birds' bony feet, stuffed them with bran to dry them, and used the grisly relics 'as purses or tobacco pouches'. After the protracted main meal of the day at four p.m., which consisted of 'one course of flesh and fowls with puddings, tarts, dried fruits and cakes', the ladies ventured on the poop deck as the sun went down, and lounged in basket chairs to watch peaceably 'the flitting shadows and light on the sails and rigging as the moon was obscured by the clouds and again shone forth'. Below them, on the quarter-deck, 'a group of sailors were dancing to the notes of a flute played by Kenny, Captain Bower's servant'.

Aired, sunned and fed again, Clementina gained strength fast, and so did her son who was a 'very plump and strong' two-month-old by the time they saw the first swallows swooping near the rigging – heralds of the land. Ten days later they took the pilot aboard and the peace of the long voyage was over. The surrounding waters were noisy with canoes of natives shouting their wares – coconuts, tamarinds, eggs and plantains – and the hammering of dismantling and packing began again. That night they finished the last bottle of port wine at dinner, Clementina saw her first firefly and heard her first jackal howling in the undergrowth along the banks of the Hooghley River.

The next day, the Indiaman, its mended sails furled for future use, proceeded in stately fashion down the Graden Reach. 'The first house of the Reach is four miles from Calcutta and from that to the city is one continual scene of woodland interspersed with a few small glades of turf and villas with ornamental grounds, and here and there a pretty little Indian cottage . . . Some of the villas are uncommonly handsome, others stiff and formal. On the opposite bank of the Hooghley are the Botanical Gardens and the handsome range of buildings composing the Bishop's College – both of these are strikingly beautiful. A sudden bend of the splendid stream brought us without preparation at once into the harbour and it was impossible to see with indifference the stately buildings of the City of Palaces, adorned as they are by the trees scattered between them – the Fort, Government House and a succession of other edifices apparently all of grey or white stone, but really of Brick stuccoed.' It was 16th November; one hundred and seven days since they left England.

Everything was strange to Clementina at first – the 'dark and glossy goat-skin water bottles' in the bathroom of their 'respectable boarding house'; the 'shuffling kind of run' of the palki bearers; the taste of custard apples and guavas; the green beams, punkahs and black marbled aisles of the Old Church where, a few days after their arrival, Baby was christened Clement Edward. The Archdeacon preached 'an excellent sermon on faith and practice as the forerunners of eternal life' and Clementina noted disapprovingly that some of the ladies in the congregation wore mittens instead of gloves.

Edward was soon allotted his place in the administrative structure: the Judgeship of Icpore at a salary of 30,000 rupees a year – about £3,000, which perhaps compensated for even the worst hazards of the voyage. Icpore was not a choice location, Clementina was warned, for the only two substantial buildings were the Judge's house and the jail, while the district contained a 'number of Europeans of indifferent class as it abounds in Indigo'. However it was only about seventy miles from the bright lights of Calcutta, which she appreciated for the first time on 30th November when the Benthalls were summoned to the Misses Edens' Thursday At Home in Government House.

Clementina had been just long enough in the country to be covered with her first layers of mosquito bites, so that she could not possibly wear short sleeves but 'contrived to make my dress answer with white satin and lace'. Two aides-de-camp met them at the entrance and escorted them to the sofas on which the First

Family was seated in a 'pretty drawing-room with crimson damask furniture and a rich carpet in the centre'. The Benthalls made their obeisances, everyone murmured something pleasant and that was that. A 'gay assembly' was dancing in the Marble Hall – such a splendid room with its floor of 'white, grey and black marble, its elegant lustre chandeliers and white pillars all chaste and delightful'. The Misses Eden continued to sit dutifully chatting on their sofas for hours, but Lord Auckland soon slipped away for a rubber of whist. He was, Clementina wrote, 'a tall, thin and gentlemanly-looking man with very marked features and gray hair. He is always very silent and seldom looks at the persons with whom he is conversing – apparently being extremely shy.'

Also, by that time, probably extremely worried, for, during the months that the Benthalls had been making their slow and fraught progress across the oceans, the news which reached Government House from Afghanistan had taken a decided turn for the worse. Rumours of intrigue and rebellion were rife and, to the perceptive and realistic British on the spot, it had become painfully clear that their presence had by no means succeeded in 'allaying all animosities' as that reckless optimist Macnaghten had predicted, but had rather exacerbated the inter-tribal conflicts in the country. In fact, although the whist-playing Lord Auckland had not yet fully comprehended it, the entire Afghan expedition was one of the most ill-conceived and ill-managed of all those undertaken by British arms in the nineteenth century.

The name of the Khyber Pass still conjures a history-book picture of curving swords, snow, bloody death, and the name of Dr Brydon, who reached Jalalabad with the tale of the massacre, is still remembered as if he were the one survivor. But there were others who lived to tell the terrible tale, and among them was Florentia Sale, wife of Sir Robert Sale, who was the commander of the First Bengal Brigade of the Indus Army.

He was a fearless, bull-headed disciplinarian but popular with his men because he was always in the thick of any fray. Florentia was his fitting mate – being also plucky, practical, tough, a seasoned soldier's wife with a sound grasp of political and military affairs that made her a critical observer of the British manoeuvres. Lady

Sale was fifty years old when she reached Kabul early in 1840; she had spent the past twenty years accompanying her husband on his campaigns in Mauritius, Burma, parts of India; on this occasion she brought with her Emily, her youngest daughter, who, the following summer, married Lieutenant John Sturt, an engineer in charge of the Public Works Department.

The women settled down quickly and competently in the alien environment, as military wives had to. They used materials from the local bazaar to brighten their bare bungalows, they cultivated always temporary gardens with plants they might never see ripen. By the second summer, her flowers were the admiration of all the Afghan gentlemen, Lady Sale said, and she was looking forward to a second autumn crop of potatoes, radishes and particularly lettuces because the native ones were 'hairy and inferior'. However it then transpired that because of the Indian Government's misguided policy of retrenchment (about half the original British force had already retired to India), her husband's brigade was ordered to leave the country, going via Jalalabad in order to quell a revolt among some stupidly unruly Ghilzye tribesmen on the way. So she was having again to forgo the crops she had planted, and prepare to join her husband.

More perceptive than most of the men on the spot, she was not sure it would be that easy. 'The Envoy was trying to deceive himself in the assurance that the country is in a quiescent state,' she wrote – and he did so mainly because he had just been offered the Governorship of Bombay and wanted to get away from Afghanistan as quickly and cleanly as possible. So, given another week or so of the fragile calm of that 1841 autumn, Macnaghten might have escaped with his head intact instead of having it swung in a chaff-bag in the Kabul bazaar, and Florentia Sale might have been spared the worst year of her life.

As it was she had her full share of horrors and disasters right from the start – which was on 2nd November. 'This morning early all was in commotion in Kabul,' she wrote. 'Shops were plundered and people were all fighting.' The insurgents, led by those tribes who were determined to overthrow Shah Soojah and get rid of the British, next attacked the British Residency, and killed the Resident. John Sturt, Lady Sale's son-in-law, sent with a message from his commanding officer to the Shah's citadel of Balla Hissar, was stabbed and carried back critically wounded to the cantonments where Lady Sale and Emily spent anxious hours swabbing blood from a wound in his throat.

Around them, within the garrison, all was 'confusion and indecision', and 'we seem to sit quietly with our hands folded and look on' – an extreme case of military inertia which, Florentia concluded, was 'in deference to the opinions of Lord Auckland whose sovereign will and pleasure it is that tranquillity and peace do reign in Afghanistan'. Orders were made and countermanded and no troops were sent out to try and quell the outbreak in its initial stages. The rebellious Afghans gained confidence and support from the British inaction and seized various strategic positions overlooking the cantonments – including the most important of all. 'Should the Commissariat Fort – an old crazy one undermined with rats – be captured, we shall not only lose our provisions but our communication with the city,' Lady Sale explained, the day before it fell.

Lacking forceful leadership or any concerted plan of action – should they defend the cantonments and/or the Balla Hissar citadel; should they negotiate a truce, abandon Shah Soojah, retreat from the country altogether – the morale of the troops fell rapidly. There was much 'roguery in the regimental bazaars' over supplies and officers started 'croaking before the men in a shameful manner'. Penned in his citadel, Shah Soojah, wishing he'd never set eyes on a British redcoat, 'lost all his self-possession and told the 860 females of his zenana that if the cantonments fell to the enemy, he would poison them all'.

Considering that the British force consisted of some 4,500 fighting men fairly well equipped with arms, their position deteriorated with incredible rapidity. Lady Sale, standing on the flat roof of her house and 'keeping behind the chimneys to escape the bullets continually whizzing past me', observed with a practised eye the various sorties and skirmishes which the British invariably lost because of bad leadership and faulty tactics. When one nearby fort was captured by the Afghans, 'a child with a stick might have repulsed them' she decided scornfully, and one gets the impression that she might often have liked to be there in the firing line showing the troops how Fighting Bob's wife could fight. But her ladyship's place was inside the cantonments, where the smell of dead camel tainted the air and the horses were so hungry they gnawed tent pegs and people grew hungrier and colder too as food and firewood supplies dwindled – and then, most ominously, the snow came.

On 23rd December, Macnaghten, who had been secretly plotting to set one Afghan faction against the other, rode out of the cantonments accompanied only by three British officers – Captain Trevor, Lieutenant Colin Mackenzie and Henry Lawrence's brother, George, – to meet the military leader Akbar Khan, son of the British-ousted Dost Mahomed. Akbar, who had foreknowledge of the Envoy's duplicity, had him murdered within sight of the beleaguered garrison; Captain Trevor was also killed in the fracas; Mackenzie and Lawrence were taken prisoner. And once again the British did nothing. The heads of the murdered men were displayed in the Kabul bazaar and Lady Sale 'had the sad office of informing Lady Macnaghten and Mrs Trevor of their husbands' assassination'. Two days later, was, she noted, 'a dismal Christmas Day indeed and our situation far from cheerful'.

After this further reverse, the British leaders seemed prepared to accept any terms, and on New Year's Day 1842 signed a treaty with the Afghan chiefs agreeing to leave Kabul at once in return for 'safe escort' to the border. Five days later the infamous retreat began, with rumours of treachery already thick in the foreboding air. Lady Sale and her daughter cooked their last hot meal with the wood of a mahogany dining-table before moving off towards the grim mountain ranges spiked between the capital and the safety of India. The progress of the once proud Army of the Indus was hampered by about twelve thousand camp-followers and about a dozen English women, several of them pregnant and with young children, some already widowed and more to be so. Florentia and Emily were fortunate enough to have their own ponies and they rode with the advance guard; most of the ladies were crammed into panniers slung on either side of camels that jogged along in the rear.

Continuous harassment, plunder and slaughter by Afghan tribesmen began almost as soon as they left the capital, and hundreds did not survive the first night. When the halt was called, Lady Sale, buttoned tightly in her poshteen (sheepskin), scraped a hole in the snow and crouched in it until, feeling herself 'gradually stiffening', she managed to beg the use of a 'straw chair' from a kindly captain. The next forty-eight hours were a long nerve-shattering nightmare as the disorderly, hungry, frightened, frozen army stumbled through snow drifts and icy streams while attacked on all sides by posses of Afghan cavalry and Ghilzye snipers. It became a panic rout, the troops abandoned their baggage, ammunition and wounded, and ran like rabbits for their lives. Florentia and Emily galloped desperately through the chaos of men, animals, whining bullets and reached the end of the first Khood Kabul pass alive. 'Fortunately,' Lady Sale commented, 'I had only *one* ball in my arm.' But Emily's husband, who had gone back to look for a missing comrade, was shot in the abdomen.

That night, the third one out, was perhaps the worst of all for the women. One Mrs Mainwaring, her horse shot from under her, ran for two miles through the icy dark carrying her three-month-old baby to reach the shelter of one of the only four tents left. Inside about thirty people were already packed, including Florentia Sale, watching her son-in-law writhing in agony. All night the blizzards howled, and bleeding, starving men tried to push their way into the shelter of the fetid tent. At dawn the ground outside was littered with the dead, and Sturt died too. 'We had the sorrowful satisfaction of giving him a Christian burial,' Lady Sale wrote.

Later that day it was proposed that all the white women and children (no one ever mentioned the hundreds of female camp-followers) should be handed over to Akbar Khan's 'protection'; this meant being taken as captive-hostages, but as it seemed their best chance of survival, the British agreed. So they were led away under armed escort to the first of many Afghan forts they would intimately and uncomfortably know. There was Lady Sale and the just-bereft Emily so 'overwhelmed with domestic affliction' that they cared little what happened next; there was the courageous Mrs Mainwaring still with her baby, the widows, Lady Macnaghten and Mrs Trevor (who had seven children and was pregnant with an eighth), two other wives whose officer husbands were allowed to accompany them, and two soldiers' wives, Mrs Wade and Mrs Burnes, who had narrowly escaped having her fingers cut off by a tribesman who coveted her rings. Among other captives were three leading officers held as hostages – Eldred Pottinger, Colin Mackenzie and George Lawrence.

Doggedly the prisoners set about exercising their British talents for survival as they were marched from one fort to another through the terrible terrain – snow-packed passes, rocky defiles, ice-laden rivers. Most of the ladies had no horses and rode behind the men. To Mackenzie's lot fell Mrs Burnes who was heavily pregnant and bundled into a sheepskin coat with the sleeves tied in front. But, says Mackenzie's biographer, 'it was only with the greatest pains he could keep her petticoats from riding up. A point on which he was especially anxious on account of the Afghans who little considered the difficulty of riding astride in a decorous fashion.' It was perhaps a somewhat minor consideration when, as Lady Sale says, the route was 'covered with awfully mangled bodies all naked; fifty-eight English were counted in the Tunghee Gorge and natives innumerable' (natives were never counted). They passed pathetic groups of camp-followers, 'still alive, frost-bitten and starving. Some perfectly out of their senses and idiotic – the sight was dreadful; the smell of blood sickening; and the corpses lay so thick it was impossible to look from them as it required care to guide my horse so as not to tread upon the bodies.' En route they were joined by the other captured leaders, Brigadier Shelton and General Elphinstone, and the whole group were eventually incarcerated in a mountain citadel at Buildeeabad. Here they were given a 'grand breakfast of dhal and radishes' and were able to wash their faces for the first time since leaving Kabul. It was a painful process – their skin, exposed to the fierce glare of snow and sun, peeled off in strips.

Buildeeabad was only about thirty miles from Jalalabad, which was still held by the small brigade commanded by Lady Sale's husband. It had stood fast there since mid-November, fighting off sporadic assaults, hearing, but scarcely believing, rumours of the catastrophes that had befallen the much larger and better equipped Kabul force. Whether or not Sale could or should have gone to their aid is still a matter of historical conjecture. He did not, but he did not retreat either and so – in that quaint manner of nineteenth-century campaigns during which some sort of post office kept going when all else failed – husband and wife were able to exchange letters between Jalalabad and Buildeeabad. 'Heard from Sale on the 22nd January,' his wife notes tersely. 'Says his force can hold out for six months.' And, three weeks later, 'A friend writes me that there will be no relief before April.'

Nor was there, nor even then; but the prisoners' living conditions improved somewhat over the months. Their three cheerless mud-walled rooms were fitted up with a few stools and string charpoys, and Lady Sale received a chest of clothes and other items from her husband which, according to other witnesses, she shared only with her daughter. Though ladies and gentlemen were compelled to occupy the same rooms at night, 'the most perfect propriety was observed,' notes Mackenzie's biographer. 'The men of the party "clearing out" as they expressed it, early in the morning and leaving the women alone.' Akbar Khan, who often visited them, sent pieces of sugar candy and chintz, over which the ladies squabbled – though it apparently went without saying that the top-ranking mems., Lady Macnaghten and Lady Sale, should have first pick of everything, while the 'women', as Lady Sale terms the soldiers' wives, should be grateful for any left-overs. Lady Macnaghten emerges from all accounts as a particularly unpleasant person. Four years before, when she and her husband were bowling along in Lord Auckland's cavalcade with no thought of their future fate, Emily Eden made caustic quips about the extravagance of her personal entourage. In captivity, she was the one who kept a trunk full of gowns for herself while other ladies had but two; Mackenzie notes that when Akbar appeared most of the ladies withdrew, but not Lady Macnaghten. And when 'in grave mockery Akbar asked her to forgive him for the murder of her

63

husband, she said she did and offered him her hand – his being, as it was, red with her husband's blood.'

At last, in early April, a relieving force under General Pollock reached Jalalabad, where the joined forces sat about for two weeks waiting for orders. Akbar, who had expected the British to advance at once, thus had time to move his captives from Buildeeabad, leaving behind the soldiers and 'women'. This was too much for Sergeant Wade's wife who, deciding she had little to lose, 'threw off her English dress and adopted a Mussalwoman's' and, 'began to consort with the Nazir of Mahomed Shah Khan'. It was too improper, Lady Sale felt, to provide more details of 'so incorrect a personage', except that she soon went off to join her 'Afghan paramour' taking with her some stolen jewellery.

The main party of prisoners was harried through the countryside, the sun's rays turning their faces 'black as Afghans', the sudden rains giving them chills and fevers. They travelled by rough mountain ponies or in cramped litters; their quarters were invariably insanitary and overcrowded, their diet an unappetizing mix of greasy mutton bones, sour apricots and chappaties made from a rough grain called ottah which was, Lady Sale said, 'a capital recipe for heartburn'. However, their relations with their captors remained reasonably cordial and she is careful to mention that Akbar treated them well by his lights – which was in the same way as he treated Afghan females.

In May they reached the lusher valleys near Kabul where corpses of Afghans, British and Hindustanis were mouldering among the wild roses, gentians, asphodel. The capital was in a state of uproar, they heard, and 'Now is the time to strike the blow . . . I hate dilly-dallying just because a handful of us are in Akbar's power. What are our lives compared with the honour of the country?' But there were other, younger, lives at stake as Lady Sale well knew. In July her daughter 'presented me with a granddaughter, another female captive', and Mrs Trevor added yet another to the group in the same week. In all, five of the British women suffered the ordeals of the retreat from Kabul and their long captivity in states of increasing pregnancy, and all survived – a testimony to the toughness of the female body. But the rigours proved too much for the elderly General Elphinstone, who died that same month, racked with gout, dysentery and visions of those terrible scenes in the Khyber for which he had been partially responsible.

By this time, of course, the British and Indian press were full of the disaster, and pundits pondered on who was to blame for how much. Extracts from Lady Sale's letters to her husband had been published and while still captive she learned that she had been cast in a Boadicea role as a leader of the troops through the Pass. This was 'folly', she explained firmly; it was 'prudence not valour' that prompted her to ride with the advance guard. Nevertheless, she was no milk-and-water damsel in distress; she always wrote what she thought and 'if people misunderstand me, it is their fault, not mine'. And what she thought now was this: whether or not the British had been justified in their attempt to oust Dost Mahomed from his kingdom was 'a matter for governor-generals and commanders-in-chief to look into whilst I knit socks for my grandchildren. But I have been a soldier's wife too long to sit down tamely whilst our honour is tarnished in the sight and opinion of savages.'

It was this spirit – which demanded some kind of 'honourable retribution' for the massacre – that spurred Pollock's force as they advanced through the corpse-littered passes to Kabul, which they reached and captured on 15th September. The prisoners meanwhile had been herded into yet another fort high in the mountain fastnesses west of the capital; much spectacular scenery, Lady Sale remarked, 'but no pleasing scene to those who expected to remain captive in that desolate region'. And, after nine months of captivity, they must have doubted if release would ever come. It did. Two days after reaching Kabul, General Pollock dispatched men of the Third Dragoons and First Light Cavalry under General Sale himself to rescue them. Colin Mackenzie noted that even the tough warrior was so filled with emotion he could not speak. As for his wife: 'It is impossible to express our feelings on Sale's approach. To my daughter and myself, happiness so long delayed as to be almost unexpected was almost painful and accompanied by a choking sensation which could not obtain relief in tears.'

But the only relief was tears for many during that troubled year of 1842, when Simla was black with widows whose husbands never did return to eat apricots and drink acid sherbert in the peaceful hills, as Emily Eden had happily imagined. Instead, the ladies found themselves having to make pathetic pleas for help to the Company in whose service their men had died: Georgina Brown, for example, whose husband Major Lewis Brown C.B. was killed in the defence of Kahun Fort. He had only a hundred and fifty men with him and the temperature was 112 degrees in the shade and the Belochees burnt all the crops in the neighbourhood and shot all who ventured outside the baking fortress walls. It must have been terrible and he died bravely, but Georgina concludes, 'Your Memorialist, instead of attempting with her feeble pen to describe in detail the services performed by her late husband and his little band of Heroes on that occasion, humbly submits to your Honourable Court the public testimony borne of their value by the Honourable Governor in Council in Bombay.'

The 'humble memorialists' were officers' wives who could at least hope to have their bereavement eased with sufficient funds to ensure their return to England and a decent, if straitened, widowhood; the ordinary soldiers' widows had no such security, and their best hope of survival was to find another husband as soon as possible. As the news from Afghanistan worsened and fatality lists lengthened, it was rumoured that some of them 'were becoming engaged three or four deep' as one memsahib put it. She, of course, was an officer's wife and wondered if, in such cases, it could be true 'that the lower classes have the same feelings as we have'.

Edward Benthall, incidentally, who was always susceptible to the ordeals of womenkind, did not ask himself that question, but donated twenty pounds that year to the fund 'For the Widows and Orphans of Camp Followers and Other Sufferers' of the Afghan campaign. The Benthalls were pleasantly settled in Icpore by then and the life offered Clementina too little excitement rather than too much. Their main diversion was to 'make up a cavalcade' with the three other British families in the town and 'go to see the Banyan' – a particularly splendid specimen of its kind growing on the plains nearby. They picnicked in its shade and Clementina tried to capture the shapes of its weird spreading in water colours. On the way home they used to visit a friend who gave them bunches of home-grown roses and a glass of fresh goat's milk for Master Baby. Baby now had a Hindu wet-nurse who insisted on having special meals at odd times and 'a very high remuneration because the job entailed a loss of caste for her'. But nurses were essential as Clementina continued to produce children – six more before she and Edward finally retired from India in 1856, which was a wise time to leave the country.

As for Lord Auckland who, with his advisers, bore the principal responsibility for so much misery, he left India with his sisters long before the full repercussions of the disastrous Afghan invasion were known. For, back in March, when the Khyber still stank with blood and the captive ladies were sitting on the cold floors of Buildeeabad Fortress, his period of office ended and he thankfully handed over the whole dreadful mess to his successor, Lord Ellenborough. 'On account of that Kabul calamity,' Emily explained to her elder sister in one of her last letters home, they did not attend the customary round of farewell dinners and dances, and 'George is looking shockingly'.

As for herself, what with it being the sixth anniversary of her arrival in this cruelly debilitating country, and her forty-fifth birthday, 'I am nearly dead of old age.' But she was not at all. Fanny and George both died six years after their return to England, but Emily lived until 1869, by which time that glittering up-country cavalcade seemed indeed a glorious pageant faded, and the Khyber Pass was remembered as just one of several blood-stained names in the story of the British in India.

PART TWO

Chapter Five

The Lawrences were lucky. Towards the end of 1842 Honoria was writing home from Ferozepore to tell Letitia, 'It was George who mended the pen I have taken in hand to begin this, beloved sister. Just fancy us all together here – Henry, George and me . . .' They had all survived, though not unscathed from that disastrous year. George, of course, had suffered trials similar to those endured by Lady Sale; Henry had spent months of non-combatant frustration when, as Political Officer at Peshawar, he had been given the thankless task of working in liaison with the Sikh forces who, after Ranjit Singh's death, verged on near mutiny. But there efforts had been rewarded by the exhilarating experience of taking part in General Pollock's advance from Jalalabad to Kabul.

For Honoria it had been a wearying time of anxiety and separation, which was, she knew, inevitable. 'A woman when she marries a soldier ought to recollect that his profession entails on her definite and often very arduous duty,' she wrote sternly in a later article that was intended to help other Englishwomen in similar Indian situations. 'Not that she has to become that most offensive hybrid, a soldierly wife . . . but she has to bear as best she may the privations peculiar to her lot and to watch against its natural fruits, which are irritability, frivolity, slovenliness, procrastination . . .'

Irritable she sometimes was, but never frivolous, nor procrastinating when it came to the duty of cheering her absent husband, to whom she wrote every day. Her heart was in a constant ache for him: 'everybody *is* in the way when you are out of it,' she told him miserably, when friends came to cheer her after his departure.

But, at the same time, she was proud of his vigorous involvement in the campaign. 'I rejoice you are there with your energy and sense,' she wrote to him at Peshawar. 'If I could but be a button on your sleeve I never would wish you to come away.' When he later offered himself as hostage to the Afghans in place of his brother George – on the grounds that George had four children, he only one – she told him that, had he gone, 'my soul would have been rent, yet I should never have wished you had done otherwise.' When he volunteered to join the march to Kabul she gallantly supported his choice: 'it would be my pride and delight to think you were even a better soldier since you had a wife and son. God forbid I should throw any obstacle in your road.' So, when Henry eventually returned safely after almost a year of separation, she had nothing to reproach herself with, she had proved a fitting mate for one whose inclinations were soldierly as well as political. 'She was a good, most good wife before, but I am innocently told that she will try and be a better one now,' Honoria wrote in that same letter to Letitia in late 1842.

Henry and George had returned from Afghanistan with Pollock's force, now termed the Army of Retribution, and, on that same barren plain where Lord Auckland had met Ranjit Singh, it was formally welcomed back to India by the British Army of Reserve, in the presence of Lord Ellenborough, the new Governor-General. The meeting was very different in kind from the spectacle of four years before – stirring in the martial manner, but also deeply poignant. Herbert Edwardes, Henry's biographer, remembered the scene well. The tents of the Reserve Army, come straight from cantonments, were 'new and white, pitched rigidly in lines like a soldiers' parade . . . traversed by broad streets, telling at once of pipe-clay discipline and the habitual peace and ease of the Indian provinces'. When their brisk bugles sounded, 'fresh-faced British soldiers and dark Indian sepoys all clad alike in the red uniform of England, bright and new with belts of spotless white' came smartly to attention.

But the tents of the army that had returned from Afghanistan were weatherbeaten, 'blown down in many a storm and chafed over many a rock'. The face of every man was deeply bronzed;

some were clothed in dirty sheep-skins with 'nothing bright about them but their musket-locks and swords'. Their bands were a mere handful of fifes, drums, bugles and their standards were torn and blackened. Nevertheless, Edwardes concludes, 'they march with the habitual step of victory and endurance, and an irrepressible cheer burst from their comrades of the Reserve as the arid plain resounded under their tread'. But neither that resounding bravado, nor the whirl of reviews, parades and festivities which, Honoria recorded, were staged to celebrate the occasion, could conceal the measure of the defeat that had preceded the 'victory', and nor could 'all the show and glitter fill up in many a lonely heart the place of those who were never to return.'

Honoria's comments reflect both the Lawrences' deep sense of disgust and disillusion with the whole British handling of the Afghan campaign, which was heightened by Henry's feeling that his own personal contribution to it was not accorded sufficient recognition afterwards. For Lord Ellenborough did not seem to know what to do with him next. In the course of 1843 the Lawrences were moved to three different districts in rapid succession, a process that was not only frustrating for an ambitious man, but troublesome and expensive for his wife, as Honoria explained. 'People at Home,' she wrote, 'can scarcely picture the small vexations of this roving life; buying things dear because we must have them; selling them cheap because we must get rid of them. Trying to carry about some few household gods; the vexation of their arriving smashed, cracked, drenched after jolting in crazy carts over unutterably bad roads, being dragged through streams – and occasionally lodged for a day or two at the bottom. At first I could have cried over the demolition of goods that I thought it impossible to do without; but every year in India my list of necessaries decreased.'

Then out of the clear blue came news that would involve them in a much more drastically far-flung move – to Nepal, where Henry was appointed the new British Resident, 'as a practical tribute to his ability and zeal,' Ellenborough explained soothingly. 'I hardly know whether to laugh or cry,' Honoria wrote to her husband when she heard. 'Then, 3,500 rupees a month is not bad;

and I say darling, *take* it . . .' Then adds wistfully, 'Do I forget that I am not to go with you?' Her question was prompted by the fact that, until then, no married man had been appointed to the Nepal post because the natives believed that if a white woman were allowed into their Empire it would collapse on the spot. Luckily, however, the Nepalese did not take their own prophecies too seriously, because, once Henry had established himself in the Katmandu Residency, he found that his wife would be allowed to go there after all – which she did with alacrity, ready as always to travel to the almost literal ends of the earth just to be with him.

Honoria 'went Dak' which was the customary method of travelling long distances before the railways arrived. 'Daks' were organized by the Postal Department which, in those distant days, was efficient – it boasted that a 'stout party' (i.e. a robust man) could go from Calcutta to Bombay in about three weeks. But, as Honoria explains, for a woman with a baby, 'dak' travelling in any degree of comfort needed preparation and forethought.

'First you must know that "dak" means post; and every ten miles or so there is a chowkee or station where fresh relays of bearers are to be found. On a civilized road there are rest-houses, ("dak" bungalows) at intervals of forty or fifty miles. To begin with you must tell the postmaster to "lay bearers" along the lines you are going. Then you see that your palki is well provided for the road. In the flat tin box on the roof – a change of clothes, a tiny box of tea, a canister of sugar and of sago, a loaf of bread, a cold fowl, two bottles of beer, a corkscrew and a metal cap, a candle-stick and wax candles. Have your medicine chest inside; oh! and don't forget to tie on the pole outside a small tin kettle, your chilumchi (brass basin) and water pot. Add this little mora (bamboo stool), useful to sit on when cooking your breakfast. And have you written to the Civilian of each district to give you a mounted guard? Have you got coppers in case you want to buy milk? Then just tie that roll of string to the palki, something will be sure to give way before long. Put your writing case under your pillow. And now you are ready to start . . .'

She journeyed mostly by night, quite alone with her five-year-old son and the bearers, who chanted quietly to each other about the conditions of the road, the weather, the local crops as they went along. It was a tribute to the Indian character that she never felt a moment's unease: 'An unprotected woman can travel safely thus from one end of India to the other,' she explained, 'thanks to the spell of the English name.' It was a grudging reason for Indian humanity, but Honoria, who often complained to her husband about the 'deep and debasing hold' of 'heathenism and idol worship' on the country could scarcely credit that such non-Christian systems had their own standards of moral behaviour.

She passed through Oudh, still a native province at that time, and its capital called Lucknow. 'Its gilded stucco and white paint has an upstart air after the marble and desolation of Agra,' she commented. 'Yet it is a curious, even a splendid city' – and the place to which her husband's name would, one day, be splendidly and fatally linked. In Oudh a 'Mohammedan gentleman' pitched a special tent for her, 'striped scarlet and white outside, with gilt pinnacles to the poles; very picturesque in bright moonlight, relieved by masses of shadow from the mango trees above.'

She crossed the River Gogra in a punt and journeyed through the district round Gorahpur where she had lived when she was first married. 'Once more I see huts made of matting and leaves shrouded with cucumber vines; so much more *eyesome* than the clay walls and tilted roofs of Ferozepore. But let me not be ungrateful to that troubled frontier where we lived at high pressure rate both of care and joy.' Thus relaxed, 'comparing old and new impressions, telling stories to my boy, I jogged along, halting at noon under a clump of tamarind trees to cook some sago.' And so, in January 1844, she safely reached the Nepalese frontier, where Henry met her with a large escort and she became the first white woman ever to be allowed official residence in the country.

After all that it is something of an anti-climax to learn from Honoria that the house she and Henry occupied in Katmandu was 'more like a gentleman's place at Home than anything I have seen out here'. It was substantial and comfortable; in its spacious grounds a real turf lawn shaded with toon trees that looked like chestnuts, and gravel walks that crackled underfoot in the home-like frosts. The temperateness of the climate, the relaxation from the hectic moving around of the previous two years restored them both to good health, and Honoria, with her man to herself at last was joyously happy. Spring brought cherry and quince blossom, the sound of the cuckoo, wild roses and soft rains; she sat on her verandah in the pale grey mornings remembering the harsh noise and glare of the Indian plains beyond the horizon, and thanking Providence for this cool, quiet interlude.

But it was *very* quiet. There were two other white men in Nepal: an Assistant Resident who was 'bullying and overbearing with a zigzag notion of truth', in Honoria's view, and a doctor who was 'ignorant and puzzleheaded'. Sometimes the isolation gave her a queasy sensation of emptiness arising from 'what is not. We know that we never *can* meet a white face outside our own grounds; never *can* have a call from a passer-by of our own colour, never *can* have a beefsteak or hear a word of English.' This would have mattered less had they been able to explore freely the almost totally unknown country, but the Nepalese rigorously guarded their secret mountain kingdom from the prying eyes of foreigners. The Lawrences were continually watched and forbidden to travel beyond the capital except on carefully prescribed routes, so that most of Nepal remained as tantalizingly 'inaccessible as the planet Venus'.

Finding themselves thus cast upon each other's company more than ever before in their married life, Honoria and Henry read and wrote articles together, discussed Indian politics and their son's future, rode among the neighbouring hills. 'I do not think we could have as much happiness anywhere in India as we have here,' wrote Honoria in the autumn of 1844. But, at that time, she was again faced with what were, for her, the real hazards of mother-hood. A second child that she had borne four years before and named Letitia, after Henry's beloved sister, had died within the year; her third, another boy named Henry and nicknamed Moggy, was, she recorded, 'the first Christian infant born in Nepal'. But that very fact added to the dangers of his arrival; the only available doctor was, as she said, 'puzzleheaded'; after the birth she fell seriously ill and was bedridden for three months, more disabled in body and spirit than ever before. Of that heavy time, she later wrote, 'In the morning I said – would to God it were evening; and in the evening, would to God it were morning.'

The load of pain and depression did not lift from her until mid-summer when suddenly she felt marvellously 'risen from the tomb', and able to go with Henry to their retreat at Koulia, in the hills above Katmandu. She responded intensely to the experience of the journey, her senses sharpened by the memory of her recent suffering. 'A lilac iris,' she saw, 'springing fresh out of a cloud of pale moss, deep blue starry blossom; scarlet berries on a shrub.' Then the joy of the Koulia house, little more than a log cabin, hung about with mist and real raindrops blistering the window panes. They ran out of bread and ate tinned biscuits from Calcutta that were 'a good deal older than Moggy and have not improved so much as he has by keeping'. The roof leaked and one sodden evening Henry ran around catching the rain 'with four umbrellas and seventeen basins'. Then the weather cleared and from their verandah she could see 'the deep yellow moon rising about the hills, lighting up the valleys of Nepal'; in the afternoons, 'a scene so perfect in its unmolestedness – the only word I can think of. All is open, spacious, boundless, but so strangely uninhabited that our bungalow might have dropped from the clouds . . . While I live, I shall always be thankful that I have seen such beauty.' Not destined for a long life, the time she had so often racked with pain and partings, she was ever aware of the wisdom of counting such blessings, for, all too soon, it was time to leave Koulia, and to begin preparations for leaving Nepal.

The health of both Lawrences was still precarious, and Henry was restless for change. He had been a competent Resident, but the small-scale, messy intrigues of the Nepalese royal court never won his true allegiance – he hankered still for a 'high pressure rate', the large issues of the north-west frontier. The Lawrences left Nepal in November 1845 and at once events overtook them. In mid-December came news that the Sikh Army had invaded British India and the first Sikh War had begun. There followed a dramatic letter to Henry from his superior, Sir Frederick Currie: 'You are required forthwith . . . The Punjab is before us. Come quickly.' Henry thundered away on horseback within twenty-four hours without a backward glance. Honoria was left to deal with a mass of unfinished correspondence and then organize her own departure for England, for it was time that Alec was sent to a 'proper' school.

When Honoria was waiting to sail from Bombay – a melancholy and reluctant passenger for Home – she perhaps reflected upon all the varieties of experience Englishwomen could have in India according to whereabouts they lived, what their husbands did, how their luck and love spun up and down. Bombay, for example, was a very different India from the regions Honoria knew best – and to come there in the 1840s as the wife of a not very successful merchant was quite a different proposition from the gritty tensions, the constant upheavals and political involvements of the north-west frontier.

The merchant's name was Sydney Terry and his wife's was Sarah, and they had four children – Amelia, Mary, Sydney and baby Freddie. Quiet, decent people, the Terrys might have been happier trading in some English provincial town, bringing up their family in a house on the Market Square, living to a pastoral old age. But they both came from families with trading connections in the Levant, and so, in April 1844, Sydney, who was already forty-three years old and had not made any spectacular headway elsewhere, decided to try his luck in Bombay, with the wholesale firm of Higgson & Caldwell.

If Sydney harboured any secret dreams of accumulating a nabob-size fortune for his family they were soon dashed. Bombay, he told Sarah (who had stayed behind in Alexandria with the children till they saw how affairs worked out), was 'the most expensive city I ever was in'. His salary was £600 per annum, but no less than £200 of that had to be deducted for life insurance, and the rest would be required to keep up even the minimum standards of a white man's life-style. 'No one walks here,' he explained to his wife, and so he was 'absolutely obliged to buy a horse for £50'. And horses required stabling and grooms, who had to be equipped with some kind of livery, harness-brushes and horsehair fly-whisks.

Then Sydney was absolutely obliged to hire a table servant because people took their own to attend them in other houses, 'otherwise they would get no attention, for the servants will only wait upon their masters'. But, alas, each servant would perform only one particular function, and so, in order to be really respectable, he had also to engage a cook, a sweeper, a boot-boy and a dhobi. The last, the washerman, quickly reduced all his linen to shreds by beating it against the washing stone in the customary Indian fashion, so then Sydney had to employ a tailor to mend it. Even then his household was extremely modest compared to some of the English residents who 'have servants to put on their stockings. I am only surprised that they do not keep men to masticate their food for them,' he told Sarah.

When the summer monsoon came he discovered that no European gentleman ever rode horseback to work in the rain, so he had to get a carriage. House rents were outrageous – £60 or £70 for two or three rooms, and 'to cut the matter short' he just could not live in Bombay under £300 per annum and was 'quite low spirited in consequence'. Nor did trade boom as he had anticipated. 'Chain cables of different sizes' sold occasionally, but the firm's cotton speculations were failing and there was a terrific wastage of goods damaged or lost in transit. But what was he to do? If he broke contract and scraped together his fare back, no one would employ him . . . So what with all that and being 'alone in a land of perfect strangers with my own sad thoughts, my heart does despond to a degree that I never thought possible,' and 'I do much regret that I ever came here.'

In these melancholy straits he desperately needed his 'dear Sally' to cheer him; he kissed her picture every night; her company would be his happiness. But he must not persuade her to come because she would undoubtedly detest the place like he did, and moreover, 'when I look round upon the European ladies that I meet and observe their unhealthy and ghastly appearance and the wan, squalid looks of the children, I feel that my wish to have you with me is too selfish. Let me at least have the consolation of knowing that you are all well.' But that was not consolation enough for long, because his miserable letters only made Sarah miserable too, till he had to start comforting her. 'If you join me here, we will, with God's mercy, contrive to live in a snug quiet way, and who knows but at the end of three years, my prospects may be better than ever they were – so cheer up again I say.'

She did – and decided to come and join him, leaving her eldest daughter, Amelia, at Alexandria in the care of relatives. The prospect bucked Sydney up at once. 'Bring a good Bonnet or two for yourself,' he told her, 'with plenty of under-linen and a good supply of stockings and shoes. White kid gloves, hairbrushes, eau-de-cologne for the steamer, and a stock of soap.' And he wanted a supply of 'cherry-stick pipes and really good tobacco from Cairo'. Sitting on his small verandah in the brief Indian twilight and picturing her presence there beside him, he told her how the frogs croaked and the crickets whirred nearby, and allowed himself the hope that she would like it after all.

And so it turned out. 'I like Bombay better than any place I ever was in,' Sarah wrote to her daughter Amelia. And why not, for – though Sydney had not noticed – the city had developed a considerable degree of European-style distinction since it had first been acquired by the Portuguese, and then by the East India Company in 1668. There was a handsome town hall, a museum and hospital, all the public buildings suitably embellished with statues of earlier British 'greats'. There was a Protestant cathedral equipped with three separate punkahs – one above the pews, one for the reading desk, one for the pulpit. These were a blessing, but Lady Falkland, whose husband was Governor of Bombay in the late 1840s, felt that the effect of a punkah hovering slowly above a clerical head distracted one from the sermon, and that the pews were 'so contracted, with their doors so unnecessarily small, that a large woman with her own breadth and the breadths of silk besides, must find it difficult to enter one of them'.

Those citizens who wished to improve themselves upon week-days also could visit the circulating library, the horticultural association, and, for the ladies, Signor Constantino Augusto's School of Art that had opened in 1822. Nevertheless, the tone of Bombay's European society was notoriously staid. One Mrs

Elwood, the first white woman on record to make the overland journey to Bombay in 1826, pronounced that social gatherings there 'were the most dull and uncomfortable meetings one can imagine'. The few ladies present sat silently on sofas, 'staring at each other,' until roused by the call to the supper table, where they drank quantities of beer and tended to doze off, like the men. Twenty years later, there were fewer than five hundred 'respectable' Europeans in the city; the men among them were said to work harder, the women to be duller and dress more simply than in Calcutta; their milieu was culturally unadventurous. As a guide-book of the time says, 'All the machinery of the fine arts is provided with difficulty, and it is therefore only among persons of extraordinary energy that their practice is continued.'

In compensation was the Bombay setting: a fine harbour dotted with monsoon-green islets where parakeets, monkeys and tame antelope were kept; its waters backed by the wooded range of the Malabar Hills and the faint blue outlines of the rocky Deccan in the far distance. The harbour, always lively with ships, was fringed by a wide esplanade, and, during the hottest months, rows of temporary bungalows and tents were erected along it for the use of European residents and visitors – for in the 1840s Bombay had but one indifferent hotel. These little dwellings, designed for coolness and relaxation, were a special feature of the city; some were of lathe and plaster, their walls lined with dungaree (a coarse, straw-coloured cloth), others thatched with date or coconut leaves, or the large dried fronds of the palmyra palm. Pallid ladies, reclining in them after lunch, would stare across the 'flats' towards the distant palm groves, yearning for the first breath of the evening westerlies to stir the tree tops and relieve the intense heat of the day. When it did, all was serene and refreshing, as one of them, Mrs Postans, remembered: 'The clean straw Chinese matting which covers the floors; the lamps shedding their soft light from the snowy ceilings, the sweet perfume of the surrounding plants and the fresh sea breeze blowing through the trellis work . . .'

Re-invigorated, one might stroll to the native bazaar near the harbour which, Mrs Postans noted, was stacked with 'piles of rich gums and aromatic spices, carboys of oil and rose water, pure ivory from the forests of Ceylon, rhinoceros' hides from the burning coast of Zanzibar and coir cables, blocks, anchors and bales of cotton'. Those in search of European fripperies and delicacies would visit the Parsee-owned 'ruination shops' inside the old Fort, and further temptations of a similar nature were pressed upon the memsahibs by the street vendors called chow-chow pedlars who arrived at their house-verandahs with baskets full of assorted desirables – Goa lace and anchovy sauce, tins of Scotch salmon, pâté, Irish butter, scented notepaper and soap, French ribbons and riding whips.

But everything was so expensive, Sarah Terry lamented to her daughter. Cheese at two shillings a pound and 'four shillings for a pair of kid gloves fit to pay a visit in', and the price of Chinese white feathers and English chintz was quite shocking. It was 'white muslin only for dinner parties, with very long sashes' – which was silly when pure Chinese silks were much cheaper in the bazaar, but 'only the half-castes wear them'. Yet somehow the Terrys had to keep up with the Jones's of Bombay where 'everyone dresses so well in their carriages, and I see all the velvet and crape bonnets'. So she too rode out in their carriage every day with the children, though it did not much appeal to her. 'How often, when as young as you are now, I wished for a carriage,' she tells Amelia. 'And now I am sick of the sight of it. A walk would be a treat. I shall forget the use of my legs.'

Even the children of Europeans were much too dignified to walk, and one lady visitor described their stately evening processional along the Bombay Esplanade. 'The women attendants are called ayahs; they wear white saris, gold bangles and nose rings. One carries a pale-faced little child in long petticoats and over the infant's head a native man servant holds a parasol; then comes a small carriage drawn by a man, and in it sits another child. The processional ends with a pony on which is a little boy. He is held on by an attendant while another leads the animal; both the young charioteer and the rider are protected from the sun by other servants carrying parasols, and thus they all creep on for an hour every evening at the same funereal pace.'

The Terry entourage was not as elaborate as that, but like others of their kind, they put up a good public front and kept their economies private. 'I am obliged to keep my accounts in good order,' Sarah says, 'as Papa looks them all over every week.' Melons could be eaten for breakfast (if they were no more than twopence each) to enliven the normal fare of rice and dried fish – the local Bombay duck. Tiffin was sometimes just marrow-bone soup, and for family dinners, 'curry and rice for ever'; though even its production was a miracle for, when Sarah first arrived, 'they had neither fork nor spoon in the kitchen, but half a coconut shell and two sticks'. To liven up the curries, Sarah made pickles of mangoes, ginger and peppers, and baked her own bread and seed biscuits. To make them all look spruce citizens, Sydney made their own polish for shoes and harnesses – with beeswax, soft soap, lampblack, turpentine. Sarah sent her Portuguese maid to the Persian bazaar to buy cheap clothing materials, but she could not go herself because only 'lower class' Anglo-Indian women shopped in the native quarters.

As time went on the Terrys learned to use the resources of their garden to the full. It was of modest size, backed by a steep hill where tamarind, coconut and guava trees grew, with monkeys sometimes swinging from one to the other. They bought twelve ducks, but the jackals who lurked in the hills ate eight of them; later they had better luck with turkeys and hens. They raised all their own house-plants – oleander, jasmine, hortensia – and Indian corn, cucumbers and tomatoes that the monkeys sometimes stole. On fine early evenings the children loved to gallop about the grounds playing horses, flying red paper kites, climbing trees to find the funny nests of the weaver birds and, when a mango fell, racing to get it before the crows did. When it was wet they played in the verandah – with toy drums and bugles, alphabet boxes and a dilapidated wooden elephant on wheels.

Mary, the older girl, seemed good at first – 'worked all day at her dolls' clothes, hemmed kitchen towels, did two lessons and a sum'. Sydney junior was a frolicking youngster who was sent to Mr Boswell's school in the old Fort, wearing his best brown holland suit and carrying his tiffin in a basket. But he was 'wild', and one day Sarah said to him, 'When you die what will become of you if you are so disobedient?' 'Why the worms will eat me and so they will you,' he replied and flew off downstairs. Soon Mary developed into a 'tomboy' too and was sent to school to keep her out of mischief. 'But I fear it is all money thrown away,' her mother declared. 'For the schoolmaster has a horsewhip and a flat piece of wood with holes in it to slap their hands . . . Good food for the body but little for the mind . . .'

Anyway the children seemed happy enough and grew fat and strong on their diet of curries and 'a wine glass of Allsop's ale every night'; but Sydney senior continued to detest Bombay. He was a plodder who obviously was not going to get to the top in his firm, though he persevered. 'Sometimes I do not speak to anyone for more than a month,' complained Sarah to her absent daughter, 'For your Papa is reading and studying Hindustani all the time he is here.' The children, incidentally, were not encouraged to follow Papa's example, for the Terrys, in common with most Anglo-Indian parents, felt that the native tongues contained so many improper words and immoral ideas that the less infant ears understood of them, the better.

A welcome break came in Sarah's humdrum routine at the New Year of 1846 when the Terrys were invited to the Governor's Ball, and, 'though we do not care about Balls I thought it right to go as many who wished to be there were not invited,' Sarah explains naïvely. The function was held in the eighty-foot-long ballroom of the gubernatorial residence at Parell, the gardens of which were illuminated for the occasion with coloured lanterns and the presence of 'two or three Natives covered with pearls and diamonds'. Parell, six miles from the Bombay Fort, was a 'decidedly pukka house', wrote Lady Falkland, who was its châtelaine in the late 1840s. She was not very fond of balls either, though she had to attend many more than Sarah Terry. At most of them there was an acute shortage of young ladies, so that, Lady Falkland wrote, she 'always knew by the expression on the aide-de-camp's face who was about to enter. He was all smiles when flowers, feathers and fans were at hand; while his face lengthened at the sight of swords, spurs and sabretaches.'

The liveliest functions therefore were at the beginning of the so-called 'cold season' in November, when Bombay residents looked forward to the latest arrival 'of a Cargo (if I dare term it so) of young damsels from England', Lady Falkland recorded. 'It can well be imagined that their age, their features, dress and manners become topics of conversation, and, as they bring the latest fashions from Europe, they are objects of interest to their own sex.' Also, of course, to the opposite sex. The gentlemen with the best chances apparently were those in the covenanted Civil Service who were obliged to subscribe to a fund which, after a time, would provide a pension of £300 per annum to their spouses if they died while in the service. Because junior civil servants usually earned an initial salary of about the same amount, they became known as '£300 a year dead or alive' men, and could thus offer most security to the cargoes of arriving damsels.

This custom of sending 'spare' young ladies out to India to find husbands was the subject of a malicious poem by Thomas Hood. It begins:

> By Pa and Ma I'm daily told
> To marry now's the time,
> For though I'm very far from old,
> I'm rather in my prime.
> They say while we have any sun
> We ought to make our hay –
> And India has so hot a one
> I'm going to Bombay . . .

And ends:-

> My heart is full, my trunks as well,
> My mind and caps made up,
> My corsets shaped by Mrs Bell
> Are promised ere I sup;
> With boots and shoes, Riverta's best,
> And dresses by Ducé,
> And a Special License in my chest –
> I'm going to Bombay . . .

As Lady Falkland was quite comfortably and securely married – to Lucius, the 10th Viscount Falkland – she customarily found her greatest pleasure in the cool early mornings after the exciting balls, when she sipped lemon tea on her Parell verandah. Below her spread flower beds, terraces, a lake, groves of feathery causarinas at the garden's end, 'the beauty of the whole scene being enhanced and enlivened by the brilliant-coloured turbans worn by the native servants', as they bustled about the first waterings.

Later in the day, as the Burra Bibi (top mem.) of Bombay, Lady Falkland had a variety of social duties to perform – such as the launching of new vessels from the Fort dockyard. The ships used to be festooned with garlands of mango leaves for the occasion, which aroused protest in the local English press about the 'ceremonies and customs of an idolatrous tendency'. Indeed, Lady Falkland owned, the launchings did involve 'a mixture of Christianity and heathenism which I am of the opinion it would be desirable to avoid', but which, she hoped, would simply fade away if she said nothing about it. As the ship left its cradle, she was customarily showered with nosegays, betel nuts and sprinklings of rosewater from the ship-builders, and handed out token presents from the Government in return.

Most of the best ship-builders were Parsees who controlled a great deal of the trading and business interests on the west coast. A tall, dignified and energetic people, they had always been popular with the British on account of their enterprise, and the first recorded Government House dinner to which native women were invited was held at Bombay in 1835 – for Parsee ladies only. Even in the cosmopolitan streets of Bombay, Parsee dress was distinctive – the men wore voluminous skirts, tight-fitting caps, and, Lady Falkland adds, a further peculiarity was that 'at the age of about seven they all put on a sacred shirt which is not worn next the skin but over the trousers; it is called the Sadra, made of a thin transparent muslin, and is meant to represent the coat of mail the men had when they arrived in India, which they were forced to abandon'.

Parsees were also distinctive in the way they disposed of their dead, who were carried to two round stone towers in the Malabar

Hills and left there to be devoured by birds of prey. 'The place is well chosen for this melancholy purpose,' wrote Lady Falkland. 'No dwelling is near; nothing heard but the waves beating against the rocks on the western shore, or the leaves of the palmyra palms crackling as the wind passes through them, nothing seen but large vultures circling in the air above.' Not being a Parsee, she was forbidden to enter the towers, but, 'being desirous of knowing how they were made', she obtained a model of one and found that stone tiers jutted from the internal walls of the roofless erections which slanted down to a circular opening at the base, 'into which bones are swept after the birds have done their duty'. Her curiosity in this regard was characteristic, for she took an unusually lively interest in her surroundings; she was also a keen water-colourist, 'perpetually seeking beautiful scenes in unknown places where no one else thinks of going', another lady wrote of her. Too charitable to preach, Lady Falkland nevertheless hinted her disapproval of her many compatriots who failed to appreciate 'the significance and value of what is constantly before our eyes', and she urged them to take up some special interest – particularly the ladies, who 'were often left so completely to their own resources'.

That was precisely Sarah Terry's problem, for she possessed little of Lady Falkland's outward-seeking intelligence, but home life did not hold many attractions either. 'My life is a dull one,' she wrote to her sister in Alexandria. 'I only see Sydney of an evening and he always falls asleep – Sydney is dull. I know it is caused by not knowing what to do regarding the children, but I take no notice – he gets no excitement, no real exercise, no society.' And what society there was is 'so dreadfully formal it is a pain to ask or be asked out to dinner'. The Terrys occasionally entertained to 'pay off old debts' that had accumulated over the humdrum months, and then Sarah supervised the making of mango and pomegranate water-ices, the killing of some of their precious fowls.

Early in their fourth year of Indian life however, things suddenly seemed to look up. They moved to a larger house that had four bathrooms, two wells and a garden large enough to grow celery, ladies' fingers, Jerusalem artichokes, aubergines, and tiger grass for the horses in the outer compound. Sydney loved it, and all that summer, as soon as he got back from work, he put on his gardening clothes and clogs and hurried outside. 'Such a dirty old figure, cutting and digging and sowing and planting.'

The last picture of Sydney. It is followed by a cutting from a Bombay newspaper dated 21st December 1848: 'Mr S. Terry. The demise of this gentleman gives another warning of the shortness of life and the suddenness of removals in India ... He was a man of much intelligence, but of quiet and secluded habits. He had for some days been suffering from a bilious attack from which no danger was apprehended when he was suddenly cut off early yesterday.' And the last words, fortunately her only recorded essay into poesy, from poor Sarah, who had made do, mended, accepted her lot with fortitude as did thousands of her kind, and who must now ...

> Check each tear, each sorrow, brave
> The desert travel and the briny wave.
> I'll not give way to unavailing woe.
> In a few days from India's shores I'll go.
> And though my heart is buried 'neath its sod,
> My hope, my trust is firm in Thee, my God.

Chapter Six

In the same year that Mrs Sarah Terry was one of the recently widowed to leave India, Mrs Helen Mackenzie was one of the recently wedded to arrive – and to see, on her first overland journey, the sublime memorial built by Shah Jahan to his dead wife at Agra. 'In the midst of the barren rugged country with nothing but tufts of dry grass and thistles to adorn the sandy plains and stony ravines, appeared the Taj, like a fairy palace in a desert, its dazzling white dome and minarets bathed in sunlight. The effect was magical.' A sight that 'makes one's chest expand and one's heart swell, it almost lifts one off the earth'. And that was praise indeed from Helen, whose feet were usually firmly on the earth and who was not prone to extravagant raptures about the romantic beauties of the East. For she was a Scottish Presbyterian, a convinced adherent of the Free Church and its moral judgements. Before she reached Delhi, she had already deplored the lack of daily worship in many Anglo-Indian households in Calcutta, declared that most of the ladies drank too much wine and were guilty of 'great carelessness in their dress – to call it by no worse name', decided that Hindu Benares was 'the very focus of fanaticism'.

But the Taj had a lesson for her. Built, alas, by heathens, it was nevertheless and undeniably one of the most beautiful buildings in the whole world, and so proof positive that the feelings which all such artistic masterpieces aroused in the spectator 'had no claim to be considered as Christian or as religious feelings at all in any other sense than as springing from those tendencies to wonder and reverence which are implanted in everyone who has a heart'. Wise indeed therefore was the act of 'our Presbyterian forefathers in stripping the worship of God of all that could delude the worshipper by exciting these poetic emotions which too often pass current for the true devotion of the heart to God'.

Having explained the matter to her satisfaction, she continued to marvel at the architectural magnificences of Delhi and its environs, which were the more joyous in her sight because she was accompanied by her husband, Colin, who knew so much about India already. Brigadier Colin Mackenzie was a veteran of several Indian campaigns. In the first Afghan War he and a few loyal Afghans had held out longest against the enemy in one of the Kabul forts and he had then 'cut his way through' to the cantonments; later he had been one of the hostages with George Lawrence and Lady Sale.

When Colin returned home after the war his name was well known, but, says Helen admiringly, 'he steadily refused to be made a lion of and declined the most flattering invitations from strangers even when conveyed by Lord Auckland'. He did not however decline invitations to visit the retired Admiral Douglas of Malvern who had two unmarried daughters. Helen, the elder, had first met Colin in 1838 when she was nineteen, he a widower of thirty-two. He had loved her then, but, on account of her youth, 'forbore to speak'. When he returned as a hero in 1843 he was irresistible and in due course they were married, at St George's, Hanover Square. The courtship, wedding and European honeymoon took some time, and when Mackenzie got back to India he discovered that his prolonged absence had been 'very prejudicial to his advancement in the political line' and 'every post was filled up'. The best that the Governor-General, Lord Hardinge, could offer, he told Colin apologetically, was the command of one of the four Sikh regiments to be raised on the north-west frontier – so that was where they were heading, with the visit to Delhi en route.

In addition to the Taj, Helen did the rounds of all the tombs, mosques, sacred wells, ancient forts and palaces, her eyes dazzled by the sheens of black and white marble; glow of red sandstone; gilded domes; walls and halls of mirrors; arches, vaults and mosaic courts embossed with traceries of silver, blue, gold. For shreds of the former glory of the Moghul Emperors still lingered in the capital, and their last descendant, the old King of Delhi, Bahadur Shah, still lived in his once magnificent palace, where he had been a pensioner of the British since 1803.

The King's estates were managed by an Agent of the Governor-General, and, at the time the Mackenzies were in Delhi, the holder of this not too onerous post was Sir Thomas Metcalfe. Just as the old King's palace reflected the grandeur of an earlier age, so Metcalfe House, near the city's Kashmir Gate, was a lavish reminder of earlier days when the top agents of 'John Company' were rich as nabobs. The residence of both King and Agent were destined for destruction in ten years' time, but in 1847, when Emily Anne Theophilia Metcalfe, Sir Thomas' seventeen-year-old daughter, came to live with her widowed father in the capital, there was little hint of impending catastrophe.

Emily was a pretty young lady of a pleasant disposition who, since her mother's death several years before, had been living in a quiet English country house. So it was rather exciting to arrive at the Indian capital in a stately gilded palanquin with a liveried escort of mounted guards and torch-bearers, and to be greeted by her father and his large retinue of household servants in a high marble hall, and to be shown to her own suite of apartments, furnished with ebony chairs, rosewood tables, ormulu clocks, silk and damask draperies. Dictating her memoirs to her own daughter fifty years later, Emily still remembered 'the wild happiness of those first days, every experience was so new and delightful and there was so much to see in every room of the house – such beautiful pictures, furniture, books and ornaments that my whole day was taken up in admiration and amazement over it'. In his Long Library Sir Thomas had amassed a famous collection of books about India; his Grand Gallery housed a unique collection of bronze busts and relics of Napoleon, for whom he had great admiration.

Sir Thomas had lived in India for about forty years when Emily joined him and he was contentedly and completely set in the ways of the country. He was a sprightly, punctilious man with lively blue eyes, 'The pink of tidiness in appearance and habits,' his daughter wrote. 'His clothes, always extremely well made by a first-class London tailor, Pulford in St James's Street, were sent out regularly each year.' He rose at five each morning, walked up and down the verandah, gave orders to the servants, took a swim in his tiled pool, said his prayers, breakfasted at eight. After breakfast his hookah was placed beside his chair; it was mounted on a solid silver stand with silver chains and a silver mouthpiece; fifty years later the gurgle of it still rang in his daughter's ears. At ten Sir Thomas ordered his carriage; on the way to it he 'passed through the row of servants . . . one holding his hat, another his gloves, another his handkerchief, another his gold-headed cane and another his dispatch box'. These items were placed in the carriage, and, with a touch of the coachman's whip to the magnificent chestnut bays, Sir Thomas was off to work, his jemadar and grooms following.

In the heat of the day Emily drifted through the stately rooms alone, played the piano or harp, read, occasionally received calls from numerous ambitious bachelor officers – some of whom arrived so regularly that she recognized the trot of their smart buggy ponies. But really 'they were generally very dull and occasionally embarrassed me by making proposals of marriage, of which of course I informed Father'. Father, she noted without malice, had instructed her to reject all such offers, and he liked obedience from his daughter. Indeed he was generally 'very particular as to the habits of ladies. He could not bear to see them eat cheese, and as for the eating of mangoes and oranges, he thought ladies ought to indulge in them only in the privacy of the bathroom.' At about three in the afternoon Sir Thomas returned home for a long, large, leisurely meal. At eight in the evening when the retiring gun boomed from the Delhi Fort, he got up, kissed Emily goodnight and walked towards his dressing-room undoing his neck-cloth and throwing it on the floor as he went.

For three years Emily lived contentedly in this essentially eight-eenth-century ambience that her father and his forbears had created. She was an affectionate daughter, a charming hostess and she did not bother her pretty head too much about all the dashing young officers who would have liked to turn it. She fell instead for a 'thin, pale, bald man, gentle in voice and manner, with mournful dark eyes full of thought and feeling' – which was her first description of Edward Bayley, an officer of the Bengal Civil Service whom she married in 1850. After the wedding she left the secluded luxury of Metcalfe House for the more ordinary, mid-nineteenth-century Anglo-Indian world where, like other women of her kind, she learned how to cope with dhoolies and gharries and cooks, how to be pregnant with dignity in a number of uncomfortable circumstances (she bore Edward thirteen children), how to make the most of whatever sudden joys out-station life offered.

Helen Mackenzie also began to learn these things when, after the grand Delhi sight-see, she and Colin travelled north-west to Ludhiana, 'reputedly one of the ugliest stations in the country'. But it was no worse than average, Helen declared stoutly – a collection of native huts, a bazaar, flat-roofed houses made of dried bricks, a few orange and pomegranate trees, all stuck on that endless sandy plain bordering the River Sutlej. The Mackenzies made their home in the compound of the American Presbyterian Mission which admirably suited Helen's spiritual and moral inclinations because all its inhabitants were Christian and teetotal. Her bungalow had a wide verandah on three sides, the back one crowded all day with orderlies, bearers, tailors, tent-pitchers, dog-boys and white-uniformed chaprassis (whose function combined that of messenger and commissionaire). In the outer compound stood a row of 'mud rooms' where the servants lived) and a kitchen-building equipped with a few brass pots, 'a kettle, a saucepan and a spoon'.

The first purchase the Mackenzies made was a cow, 'a high-class looking creature with head and legs like an Arab horse, eyes like a gazelle, a deep hanging dewlap and a hump between her shoulders which is very becoming'. Later they acquired sheep, quails, ducks, hens and two long-eared Punjabi goats which fed out of Helen's hand; after the dawn gunfire, the day's next sound was of their awakening. While Colin rode off to morning parade, Helen took a stroll on the flat house-roof and watched the routines of the day begin. Sad-eyed, creamy bullocks, prodded by their drivers, began to plod up and down to draw water from the well, and this was channelled into the water-courses that ran round the newly-planted trees in the compound and the beds where roses, vegetables and barley grew. The camels tethered round the guards' tents snorted for breakfast, and the sweeper let the fowls out of their bamboo coops. The ducks quacked and paddled in the water as it flowed, and the house-servants hurried to and from the kitchen with fresh-baked chappattis.

When all too soon, the cool of dawn evaporated, Helen went to unlock the store-rooms and dole out to the servants the daily allowance of flour, sugar, potatoes and rice and give instructions for dinner. Then she rode elephant-back to the parade ground to accompany her husband back for 'chota jazari' (little breakfast), '. . . that most sociable of all Indian institutions, when intimate friends drop in for tea or sour curds and chat until the heat drives everyone into the house'.

Naturally, most of the chat was about the setting-up of the new regiment, which, fortunately, Helen found as fascinating a subject as did Colin. The first Sikh War, to which Henry Lawrence had ridden hot-foot in December 1845, had been a brief campaign. The Sikhs were defeated in the spring of the next year, another Sikh–British settlement was made and Kashmir became an independent state. Henry Lawrence was given one of the jobs he had always wanted – British Resident of the Punjab, stationed in Lahore with the prime task of re-establishing peace and order in the troubled Sikh kingdom. In furtherance of this he reduced the divisions of the former powerful Sikh Army and ordered the setting up of smaller, tightly disciplined forces, part Sikh, part Afghan, part Hindu, who would, hopefully, be loyal to the British.

This was why Colin Mackenzie had the difficult task of raising and drilling the Fourth Regiment Frontier Brigade. His main problem was the chronic shortage of money, supplies and efficient, experienced personnel that beset the whole Indian Army at this period; during the 'little breakfast' chats, these deficiencies and grievances were thoroughly aired. The Ordnance Department sent Colin some 'wretched old muskets which were only fit to be broken up', so he sent them back; he issued proclamations asking for local recruits, but as the pay and conditions of service were poor even by native standards, and most of the able-bodied men were busy with the harvest anyway, it was mainly the 'refuse of the region' who applied. Colin's Adjutant proved to be half-literate and wholly drunk so that Helen spent part of her time keeping the regimental accounts and copying out dispatches. But the worst headache was the niggardliness of 'H.Q.', and the Mackenzies felt like giving up the whole endeavour when Colin applied for 'hutting money' to repair the native quarters in 'the lines' and was told that the men must pay for it themselves.

'The Lines' – what untold misery was contained for so many for so long in those two little words. Each company of each regiment had its own lines – rows of brick and plaster barracks for the English soldiery, huts for the native infantry. Commonly, the quarters were overcrowded, sparsely furnished and poorly ventilated; usually they also stank, having been built close to ravines which, as one staff surgeon of the time, Julius Jeffreys, put it, 'become the depositories of what more refined communities are at such pains to carry off by sewers'. When they were not on active duty, the men were frequently confined inside these buildings for most of the day, and, as Jeffreys says, 'If anyone would see a picture of the gnome Ennui reigning absolute, not even the descriptive power of the poet Spencer will so well supply it as the scene within a barrack compound in India surrounded by a hot, dull, mud wall.'

If it was that bad for the men, what must it have been like for the wretched Englishwomen, the lowest in rank and least remembered of all the 'mems.', who chose, or were obliged, to accompany their menfolk for the ten-year stint on the hot hell of the Indian plains? Officers and travellers glimpsed them – jolting along in bullock-carts from one barracks to another. Arrived at a new post, the soldiers' wives went off to haggle in the native bazaars and the officers' wives shuddered to see them – as they did to hear them carolling drunkenly from the canteen occasionally, or keening over their dying children. For 'the mortality of the barrack children is appalling . . . The infanticide of the Hindu is not more indefensible than the treatment of these poor little ones – it is a process of 'protracted liquidation' of our own English stock,' thundered Jeffreys, one of the few doctors who noticed.

Exposed from birth to the harshness of the Indian climate, fed on a diet of often sour black bread, unclean fruit and 'bazaar pork' (from the swine who were driven to forage in those unwholesome ravines), it was not surprising that many children died, nor that many of their mothers turned to alcohol for temporary oblivion. 'The soldiers' wives,' says Mrs Postans, one of the few travellers to have commented on them, 'are not content with frequent libations of raw arrack; they boil in it spices and green chilis to increase its potency, and give smaller portions of this deleterious compound to their children who are seen rolling in the dirt and squalor about The Lines exposed to the deadly influences of the tropic sun.' They, and their husbands, would have been well advised, she felt, to assimilate a few of the humbler habits of the sepoys, whom she used to see on her evening rides near the native lines, 'baking their badjares cakes on the bright wood fires for the family meal, or playing with their little urchin children in quiet domestic enjoyment'.

Not even the English soldiers who endured similar conditions could find much to say for their female compatriots. Sergeant R. Waterfield, serving in the Ludhiana district with the 32nd Foot at the same time as Colin Mackenzie, deplored their disorderliness – and other frailties. When their husbands were away and there was no one to 'watch over them or keep them within bounds, they come out in their true colours and prove false to all their plighted vows. There were some exceptions, I am afraid but few, and the scenes enacted by the false ones were in some cases disgusting in the extreme. So much for matrimony!' In short, women on The Lines were 'more trouble than they are worth. When they are on a march, they are very humble and are glad to get some of the men to help their hackeries over the nullahs or ravines, but once they get settled in quarters, they turn up their noses to you and get quite saucy and full of dirty pride. If I could do anything in it, I would make them wash clothes for the men, as they do at home.'

And perhaps some of the poor creatures did behave childishly – for one thing, as Honoria Lawrence noted, some of them were little more than children. She recalled one such – a pallid, skinny youngster who said that her corporal husband often beat her because she 'stayed out playing marbles with the boys when he wanted his supper'. Barrack girls were often married off in their early teens to men much older than themselves about to go on active duty, because, one told Honoria, 'if he's killed I'll get six months widow's pension'. And then there would always be other men ready to take her, for white women were rare in the ranks. Considering this, and that they were forced to live in the communal rooms 'among drunken and half-naked men, hearing little but blasphemy and ribaldry, and surrounded by influences that render decency nearly impossible', it was, Honoria realized, inevitable that the soldiers' womenfolk earned and kept their bad reputation.

As Colin Mackenzie's regiment was of native infantry few white women were attached to it, but those few fared as badly as the rest. 'A poor soldier's wife is indeed to be pitied,' wrote Helen, after talking to the wife of a bombardier who had lived on tea and chappattis for two months on a journey from Calcutta to Cawnpore, during which several of the other wives died of sunstroke or cholera. 'She is often a young and inexperienced country girl, nobody cares for her, no one looks after her; her health is as likely to give way as any lady's in India; she is treated more like an animal than a woman . . . She is sent hither and thither at all seasons and she may truly say, "No man careth for my soul" – for even the army chaplains were reluctant to offer them any consolation. But Helen's sympathy too remained at a distance and she, like the great majority of officers' wives, felt she had done her duty by the other ranks with the arranging of a Christmas Party for the barrack children where they could stuff themselves with oranges, buns and sweetmeats.

Helen was more constructive, however, in the help she tried to offer several, formerly wealthy Afghan families who, following the war in their country, had been sent into exile in Ludhiana because of their pro-British sympathies. They had been promised rewards for their loyalty, but were now reduced to near penury. Colin Mackenzie, who, like Henry Lawrence, had been a severe critic of the British policies in Afghanistan, was furious at the treatment they received and constantly urged the authorities to remedy the situation. Because, therefore, Colin was held in exceptionally high esteem by the Afghans, Helen was able to get on a footing of unusual trust and familiarity with their women-folk.

They lived in a one-storied mud-wall house with no windows, their only escape being to an inner courtyard, where they lolled about on padded red and yellow mats. Helen ministered English medicines and readings from the Bible to them, ate mutton kebabs out of the communal dishes, began to realize the jealousies and miseries of their cloistered lives. She learned enough to 'refute authoritatively . . . the fine theories of Mr Urquhart regarding the superior happiness of Muhammedan women . . . What *can* a man know of the matter? . . . Had he friends and acquaintances in half a dozen zenanas?' *She* had, and knew that what caused 'heart-burns innumerable' was the institution of polygamy. 'It is not in human nature to be content with being only a fourth part of a man's wife,' she asserted, watching how the favourite women, bangled in silver and gold, were pampered by their Khan, and how the unfavoured cowered in corners, their eyes spiritless or spiteful.

As for the rest, their secluded lives 'are hardly more devoid of excitement than I am myself', she realized, as she settled into the monotonous regularity of her situation. She read the Scriptures to her favourite servants and, encouraged by the two who became Christian converts, she tried to start a little school for their children, but 'had the greatest difficulty in persuading them that they are sinners'. Sometimes she mounted one of the regimental elephants and went off for a little sketching, a rewarding occupa-tion in a somnolent land, for, 'all creatures in India appear to me much better sitters than at home and have a greater faculty for keeping still . . . The very birds sit tranquilly and meditate on their spray.'

In April the heat began; the sky, the corn, the skins of the Anglo-

Indian children turned white with it. Time to get the punkahs out of storage, oil and repair their frames, mend the tattered flounces of calico, renew the edges with turkey-red binding. By 2nd June, Helen noted, 'Thermometer eight-seven and a half with Punkahs and Tatties'. The buffalo butter was put in the thermantidote to keep cooler. It became a matter of skill, as another mem. with experience of 'hot-weather housekeeping' put it, 'to grasp the fleeting moment between toughness and putrefaction when the joint may possibly prove eatable'. All day the house remained barricaded tight; in the dim light the only sounds were the occasional pad of a servant's bare foot, the click of the punkah-rope. Outside the brazen sun grinned mercilessly from the cloud-less sky; the earth cracked in torment; the only sounds were the creak of a bullock-driven water-wheel, and the occasional croak of a crow gasping on the branch of a withered bush. Even after sunset, Helen complained, 'the hot wind is as scorching as if you were standing close to a huge kitchen fire'. The winds brought storms of dust, dense enough to obliterate even the brightest sun, and send them all 'groping about for lights at midday'.

In such summers ice was as precious as gold and similarly hoarded. During the nights of the previous mid-winter, shallow saucers were filled with water and placed in beds of straw on the open plains. The ice that formed was collected just before dawn and stored in deep pits. When the heats began it was dug up, still solid, and quickly sold to members of the regimental 'ice-club' to put in their lemon tea, fruit drinks, brandy and sodas. When the rains came in late July the air cooled slightly; swarms of flying ants appeared and shed their wings all over the floors, to be wafted into drifts by the punkah's breeze. Outside, small ponds glinted again among the sandy wastes and the garrison elephants wallowed about in them after their day's work, while their mahouts stood on their sides to scrub them down.

Helen's personal elephant was equipped with a 'movable canopy' of thick curtains fixed on poles around the normal howdah to keep out the worst of the driving rain or dust. It was obviously a tractable beast, but elephants in general were prone to bouts of irritation which they expressed by puffing themselves out to such a size suddenly that their howdah ropes burst; then they shook themselves vigorously – and down would come Sahib, howdah and all.

At sunset, Helen and Colin often rode elephant-back along The Lines, which had been greatly smartened up with neat broad-walks, young trees planted round the wells and huts of sun-dried brick. But the maintenance of The Lines was only one of Colin's problems. It took six months for consignments of arms to reach Ludhiana from Calcutta, and, as a commander did not get his own pay in full until the men of his force were fully equipped, some of the officers had to borrow money to keep going at all. Nor were they all able to conceal their difficulties, for, as Helen said, 'one learns to know people in India most thoroughly. Everyone lives, as it were, in a glass case. Everyone knows the income, style of living, debts and position of everyone else.' When straits got really dire, families traded items of furniture among themselves and some of the officers' wives were constrained to part with their most prized possessions. At such times, Helen remarked caustic-ally, 'women calling themselves ladies can be found who will beat down the price of any jewels sold and get them for half their value'. The Mackenzies were not so severely reduced, but they, like everyone else, were most relieved when funds finally arrived and the sepoys lined up on the verandah to receive their allow-ances, with sweetmeat-sellers standing by to tempt some rupees from them at once.

By the summer of 1848 the regiment was getting into its stride, and Helen got a great thrill from watching their parade exercises. 'A fine-looking corps – about five-eighths of them being Sikhs and Afghans, they are capable of thrice the work of a Hindustani regiment.' She was touchingly proud of Colin's natural 'air of command' and the loyalty he inspired. 'His men do whatever he desires of them,' she wrote. 'There is no doubt that when soldiers behave ill it is almost always because of their officers.' Mackenzie was popular partly because he tried not to offend the men's national customs; he had special 'Glengarry bonnets' made of 'a very soldierly appearance' and high enough to accommodate the Sikhs' long, luxuriant tresses. Helen helped to make the rosettes for them and to design the regimental colours – rich yellow with a small Union Jack in the corner and a wreath of oak leaves. It was a happy day when she presented them to the regiment on the parade ground, with Colin riding by her side and explaining to the men what a great honour it was for a lady to grace the occasion with her presence, at which everybody formed lines and saluted everybody else 'most beautifully'.

It was as well the regiment had been pulled together, for during most of 1848 there was increasing restiveness and disaffection in the Punjab. Early that year Henry Lawrence had been sent home on sick leave to join the waiting Honoria and, while he was away, an anti-British revolt – the Second Sikh War – broke out, centred on the cities of Multan and Lahore. According to Henry's admirers, it was mainly due to his absence at this crucial time that the British on the spot delayed taking effective action, and Colin was one of many officers who chafed at the delays and begged to be allowed to join the fray, even as a volunteer. When he finally reached the battlefield he was appalled at the situation and wrote to Helen that 'here we are in such a mess as the Army of India has never been in since the days of Clive'. Soon after writing that, Mackenzie learned that Henry, having also heard how bad things were, had made one of his mad dashes back to India and had joined the Governor-General's camp at Ferozepore; so Mackenzie hurried to meet him, feeling they shared the same sense of urgency. As things turned out however, Lawrence was not given the commanding position he had expected because he never established the same rapport with the new Governor-General, Lord Dalhousie, as he had enjoyed with his predecessor, Lord Hardinge. He had thus left Ferozepore when Colin arrived, and it was not until the final defeat of the Sikhs a few months later, when the air throbbed with rumours about the coming annexation of the Punjab by the British, that the Mackenzies and Lawrences finally met.

During his leave Henry had been made a K.C.B., so it was Lady Lawrence to whom Helen was introduced and with whom she pronounced herself 'very well pleased'. Honoria told Helen that her recent stay in Lahore had been 'like keeping a table d'hôte without being paid for it', and added that, nowadays, she 'hardly ever saw her husband quietly'. Apparently the basic drawbacks of being married to a man like Henry had not diminished with the years, and Honoria's description of them was persuasive enough to convince Helen that no 'amount of pay or rank can compensate for the loss of domestic life, especially for two people who seem so attached to each other'. For it was, she thought, 'very beautiful' to see the degree of the Lawrence family's mutual affection. 'There was no hint of jealousy between the three brothers, and their wives love each other like sisters.'

Honoria had some justification for complaining about the long and weary separations from her husband, for she had not long returned to India after more than two years alone in England. She had spent part of the time selecting staff to teach at the Hill Schools which she and Henry established for the families of British soldiers in India. It was typical of the large-hearted Lawrences that they should have been among the first to be moved into doing something for those 'poor white barrack children' whose plight Dr Jeffreys described; it was typical of their impulsive generosity that they should spend so much of their personal money on the first school that John Lawrence, the hard-headed businessman of the family, was called in to set their finances in order. The school, called the Lawrence Military Asylum, had been opened at Sanawar in 1847 and was a product of its founders' evangelism. The Mackenzies visited it on the way down from Simla and Helen was much impressed with 'the healthy rosy English-looking girls' compared to those on the plains. Colin cross-examined the boys and found they read and answered well and 'what pleased him most was their respectful open manner. They are evidently well *trained* as well as taught.'

Soon after their return to Ludhiana, the Mackenzies learned that they were being posted away from the north-west altogether, and resolved to pay a short visit first to Lahore, where they again met the Lawrences. In the spring of 1849 Lord Dalhousie had decided that the recently-annexed Punjab should not be ruled solely by Henry, its former Resident, but by a Board of Administration, consisting of Henry as President and two other members – his brother John, and a civilian, Charles Mansell. The decision was a bitter blow to Henry and was soon to cause much controversy and discord, but in the early days of its existence, when the Mackenzies visited Lahore, the Lawrence brothers and their wives were living together in the old Residency and the arrangement seemed viable.

For Henry it was another peiod of that 'high pressure' anxiety and industry on which he actually thrived. His staff of 'young men' – several of whom became famous as the next generation of soldier-administrators – were almost expected to succumb periodically to 'Punjabi headache' caused by overwork. As for the women, those who married into the Punjab Commission had 'taken a step as decisive as entering a convent', in the view of a contemporary historian. 'She and her children become camp equipment, jolted in bullock-carts and on the backs of camels, exposed to dust, sun, heat, cholera and malaria, moving always from tent to bungalow and back again, gypsies without a home hearth beneath the stars. They must expect hard wear and a short life, and, if they survive that, years of anxious, deadening separation. To accept such a life without some sense of spiritual dedication would almost inevitably mean a coarsening of the fibres, but the wives of the Lawrences and their followers were vowed to God just as definitely as their husbands, were as closely knit in a community of work and religion.'

And certainly Honoria had that air of moral strength and security about her which her husband's 'young men' admired and loved. One of them wrote of her later: 'She was not beautiful in the ordinary acceptance of the term, but a harmony, fervour and intelligence breathed in her expression.' Her demeanour was not, however, forbidding, for says her biographer, Maud Diver, she 'delighted the hardworked youngsters by her zest and Irish humour, her appropriate nicknames, her disregard of the conventions . . . Her room – where any of them were welcome at any time – became a rallying point for all the wit and talent among them. Her informality set the shy at ease. There was no trace in her of the official Burra Mem, genuine helpmate as she was of the most unconventional Burra Sahib in India; so careless of externals that he would have gone almost in rags without a woman to look after him.' Henry called himself the worst-dressed man in India and his wife had but little more sartorial concern. When the increasing heat made stiff close-fitting gowns a burden, she went about comfortably in 'a long grey flannel petticoat and high-necked cotton bodice', which was, in Helen's view, 'perfectly decent of course but not presentable'.

It was the Lawrences' practical, no-nonsense evangelism that prompted Henry to establish a Soldiers' Garden when he was in Lahore. Helen described it as being laid out with much taste – vegetable- and flower-beds, rustic seats, a labyrinth, open ground for gymnastics and racquets, a menagerie with two or three tigers, a coffee shop at the entrance. Fêtes were held there, football games and donkey-races, and the soldiers' wives brought their children to eat buns on the grass and watch the tigers being fed. This creation of a home-like sort of place in the alien Punjabi city was, Helen concluded, 'most creditable to its generous founder'.

For that was Henry's way – he was a very benevolent patriarch, but of autocratic temperament and he never could reconcile himself to 'being a Board', as another autocrat, Lord Dalhousie, wrote of him. To try and ease the tensions, Honoria and Henry moved from the shared Residency in 1851 to a delightfully unusual house built round the tomb of Muhammed Kazim, a cousin of Akbar the Great. It was a single-storeyed octagon with an outer octagon of bathrooms and verandahs overlooking the plains outside the city. Honoria loved its airy, bare, high rooms, its remote quiet. 'I can be out of doors as much as I like without meeting anyone,' she wrote to Alec, at school in England. 'I can mount my pony and toddle about to my heart's content.'

But for Henry there was no such respite from the cares of office and he found himself frequently and bitterly at odds with both his brother and Lord Dalhousie over Punjabi policy until, in late 1852, he resigned in frustration. Dalhousie, whose sympathies had always been with John Lawrence, accepted his resignation with relief, and gave Henry instead the position of Agent in Rajputana. Some men would have rejoiced, but for Henry it simply meant exile from his beloved Punjab and '£6,000 a year to watch the wayward fancies of a score of effete princes' – a lesser Nepal all over again.

As in Nepal, there was for Honoria an unexpected period of quiet content to be snatched there. The Residency at Mount Abu in the Aravalli Range was 'perched on a granite rock', she told Alec. 'From our bedroom is a door leading into the little thatched verandah and out in to the tiny garden. Here I greatly enjoy sitting, looking down into the lake, surrounded by rock and wood. I like watching the kites sailing in circles and busy little swallows skimming among them unmolested. Then we have a lovely little humming-bird that hovers like a butterfly over a flower, plunges in its long slender beak and sucks honey.' But the greatest happiness, she told him, was the 'enjoyment of your Father's society such as I have never known since we left Nepal'.

Hopefully, like the humming-bird, she sucked all the honey from those days, for they were among her last. She was forty-five and looked much older, for Henry and India between them were fast wearing her out. 'The condition' she had often dreaded and suffered through was again upon her, and this time it simply drained the last of her life spirit from her. She knew it would, shielded Henry from the truth as long as she could, and died. Henry's biographer paid tribute to one whose task had been 'to cheer, stimulate and help the upward struggles of an earnest man, to lend grace to the strength of his career, and to trim with faithful hand the lamp of the spirit shining on his work'. The struggling man, left alone, wrote to his sons on the day of her death of 'her lovely and loving influence', reminding them that 'few boys ever had such a mother'. The day was 15th January 1854; in the light of what Henry then lost he would the more readily face his own death three and a half years later, when the storm broke.

Chapter Seven

To say that the storm of the Indian Mutiny – more accurately, the Sepoy Revolt – at last gave the English memsahibs something to write about is not to minimize its horrors but to place them in perspective. For those women who were living in parts of central and northern India in certain cantonments at that particular time, the experience was searing. Some did not survive it; those who did were thrust hard against the barbarities of war and the harshness of ordinary Indian existence for the first time. They suffered extremes of thirst, hunger, fatigue; they shuddered at the close whine of bullet, the crump of shell; and they remembered those dreadful days for the rest of their lives – and so wrote of them, partly to neutralize and contain the terror of it all, as people do.

For the female majority who were living in the three main Indian cities or in the hill-stations, the Mutiny remained no more than a nightmare story and they could scarcely believe that it was actually happening. Those to whom it did happen could hardly believe it either. The English civilians who came in daily contact with the peasantry had no prescience of it; the army officers living right in The Lines could not imagine that their loyal and disciplined sepoys, of whom they were truly proud, would actually rise in revolt against them. And if the men could not conceive of it, how much less could the women, who experienced the country mainly through their husbands, who were cosseted and debarred from most real investigations of their own, who relied, by upbringing and custom, on the infallibility of the masculine judgement?

So, in most of the women's accounts, there trembles a note of utter incredulity, an innocent and instinctive rejection of the evidence before their very eyes: that filthy, shrieking, dying babe, could it possibly be little blonde Emily whose amah was wheeling her through the Botanical Gardens in a pram two months ago; that shattered, legless corpse, could it actually be, have been, young Miss P. . . . who skipped merrily through every cotillon at the last Christmas Ball?

The first British women to die violent deaths were those unlucky enough to be in Meerut, a town forty miles north of Delhi, on the night of 10th May 1857. It was the largest military station in the north-west provinces, with the highest proportion of British to Indian troops, which should have made for safety. But the idea of safety proved illusory when, early that Sunday evening, hundreds of sepoys of the Third Cavalry and 20th Native Infantry regiments grabbed their swords and rifles and went savaging through the bazaars, burning the bungalows of The Lines, and firing and slashing at every white face they saw. It was all over very quickly. The British officers, stunned into confusion and indecision, did not rally their forces fast enough to quell, or even contain, the outbreak; the sepoys, anticipating more organized and sterner reprisals than they actually got, realized there was no future for them in Meerut and clattered off in their hundreds towards Delhi, full of ambitious plans for fermenting a large-scale national uprising.

Dawn of the 11th revealed rows of gutted bungalows in the shattered garrison, and a number of shot, mutilated, burned corpses of English people. Meerut's Commander-in-Chief, General Hewitt – branded ever after as the foremost example of the incompetence and ineptitude that turned out to be quite common among the ageing men in charge of the Indian Army at the time – simply ordered his men to clean up the mess and be prepared to defend their cantonments against all comers – who never came. He sent no force in pursuit of the insurgents, nor did he instantly alert the rest of the country to the disaster. Perhaps he could not quite believe it – according to one contemporary historian, he had 'drowsed and nodded through some fifty years of routine service in India . . . rising by mere seniority to his present position'. After all that time, and when he had come thus far, how could such a catastrophe happen?

Its immediate trigger-cause was known to General Hewitt, of course, as to everyone in the garrison: that the sepoys of Meerut had refused to use the cartridges for the recently issued Enfield rifles. Before these cartridges could be rammed down the barrel, they had to be greased and their thin paper ends bitten off. It was rumoured that the grease was a compound of pork and beef fat, and to the thousands of Hindus and Moslems these animal fats were unclean. Several of the native regiments had been faced with these new weapons, and complaints, rumours, fears had been stirring in the ranks for several months. At Meerut the situation was handled in a particularly short-sighted and bull-headed manner. Brevet-Colonel George Smyth of the garrison's Third Cavalry determined to demonstrate to the men that the hated cartridges were harmless, and could, in any case, be torn rather than bitten before use. He lined his troops on the parade ground and ordered them to prepare to fire the Enfields. Eighty-five sepoys refused. They were court-martialled for mutiny and, in front of their comrades, had their uniforms stripped off and were fettered in irons. That took place on 9th May; the next day the revolt began.

But there were several other more long-term and substantial discontents that had been fermenting in parts of British India for some considerable time. 'The causes of insurrection,' wrote Francis Bacon, 'are innovation in religion, taxes, alterations in laws and customs, breaking of privileges, general oppression, advances of unworthy persons ... factions grown desperate, and whatsoever, in offending people, joineth and knitteth them in a common cause.' He could have been describing India at the time of the Mutiny, when Hindu and Moslem joined in their opposition to the greased cartridges and in their more general fear that the introduction of them was part of a widespread British plot to undermine their customs of religion and caste; when the traditional privileges of many wealthy landowners and minor princes had been disregarded or eroded by the policies of annexation carried out by Lord Dalhousie; when there had been many 'advances of unworthy persons to positions of authority that led to discontent among both British and Indians; when there was a good deal of oppression of the native population by Anglo-Indian military and civil personnel who had grown lax in their discipline and standards of behaviour.

Add to these factors that it was the year 1857, just a hundred years after the Battle of Plassey, and popular hearsay had it that British rule in India would last for a century. Add, too, the growing pressures of industrialization, social innovation and aggressive Christianization which the Western nations were beginning to impose on the whole of the East, and all the likely occasions for seditious rebellion obtained. In defence of General Hewitt therefore, it could be said that if the Mutiny had not begun at Meerut on that Sunday in May, it would have begun soon somewhere, and that, given the generally ineffective and inefficient leadership of the Indian Army at the time, the rebellion was bound to gather the rapid and unchecked momentum it did.

The initial momentum carried the first bands of dissident sepoys to Delhi because that was where the old King Bahadur Shah still held his empty courts. As the surviving symbol of the once-powerful Moghul dynasty, they hoped to hail him as the new Emperor of Hindustan; under his banner, Moslem and Hindu were willing to rally together and free India from the foreigners' hated yoke. In Delhi itself the yoke did not chafe so very harshly, for the British, respecting in an offhand or cautious manner that the capital was the cultural centre of the former Indian Empire, did not flaunt their presence. No large contingents of British troops were stationed there, and the cantonments two miles north of the city contained regiments of native infantry, commanded by a few British officers. There were some permanent British civilian residents of course – a commissioner, some senior civil servants, bankers and merchants, and Sir Theophilus Metcalfe, nephew of Emily's father Sir Thomas, who had died, reputedly of poisoning, four years earlier.

One of the officers in charge of the 38th Bengal Native Infantry was Captain Robert Tytler, a Scotsman who had seen service in the First Afghan War, and who was married to Harriet, a colonel's daughter who had been born in the country. She was a cultivated and able woman who was enjoying their Delhi assignment; she and Robert were planning to publish a book about the antiquities of the old capital, for which she had already executed several paintings. The Tytlers did not entertain a great deal, being content with their own company and that of their children, four-year-old Frank and two-year-old Edith, and they were looking forward to a new addition shortly. At eight a.m. on 11th May they were eating melons for breakfast, as was usual for the time of year, in their cantonment bungalow on the Ridge, the high barren line of hills that overlooked the city. As usual, it would soon be scorchingly hot; from the outlying streets below there rose, as usual, the sounds of trundling carts, cries of water and vegetable vendors, squawks of rooftop crows. Suddenly the tailor, who had been squatting on the verandah outside, sewing as usual, burst into the room shouting, 'Sahib, sahib, the army has come.' It was many weary months before there was another usual moment in Harriet's life.

Robert had heard rumours of threatening trouble, though he, like everyone else in Delhi, was still ignorant of the previous night's outbreak in Meerut, and he rushed off to join his commanding officer at the barracks. Harriet paced the verandah, looking anxiously towards the city, while the servants muttered together, avoiding her eyes. Soon she heard the unusual sounds of bells, bugles, clattering of gun-carriage wheels; then a message arrived saying that all non-combatants were to leave their homes at once and make for the Flagstaff Tower on the north side of the Ridge.

When she, the children and their French maid Marie reached the Tower, they found other frightened and bewildered ladies who told her the dreadful news – some two thousand mutineers from Meerut had poured into the city that very morning and were killing every Christian they could find. The British Resident of Delhi, the Captain of the King's Guard and several English civilian families were already slaughtered, and the outlook for the rest of them was grim. Harriet put her arm protectively round little Frank; he had blue eyes and a very fair skin; in her mind's eye she saw a sword slashing through that white young throat.

As the tense afternoon wore on, the ladies, armed with rifles, crouched together in the Tower's upper storey and strained to hear the sounds of a relieving force, which, everyone assumed, would soon arrive from Meerut. None came; instead a bullock-cart loaded with the still bleeding corpses of slaughtered British officers was trundled to the Tower and left in the courtyard. It was Robert Tytler, shaking free of the paralysis of sheer disbelief which seemed to grip most officers in their first hours of Mutiny experience, who set about mustering the support of his still loyal sepoys and planning a retreat from the city. 'We must fly for our lives,' he told the ladies – it was as simple and incredible as that.

All available transport was commandeered and, when twilight fell and the noise of fighting diminished, Harriet with her brood and Mrs Gardiner, the Adjutant's wife, with hers, all squeezed into a small buggy and made for the Kurnal road. Looking back towards the turbulent capital, Harriet saw with a sinking heart that the cantonment bungalows were all ablaze; everything they owned had gone. 'The relics of a beloved child who died, manuscripts and paintings for the book, furniture, books, carriage and horses – all amounting to over two thousand rupees – a fortune for a military man in those days.' Also ablaze that night was Metcalfe House, among whose stately rooms Emily Anne Theophilia had happily drifted ten years before. The rebels stripped its copper roof, demolished its marble statues, carried away those prized relics of Napoleon, and burnt Sir Thomas' famous library – which was a shame because it contained many rare books on Indian history.

The flight from the ransacked city was terrible. There were so many people packed into the buggy that its wheels broke under the strain. Robert and Captain Gardiner commandeered a bullock-cart for their wives, who were both heavily pregnant, and its rough jolting over the unmade track was sheer agony. It took them several days to reach the comparative safety of the large military station at Ambala, by which time their clothes were in rags and they were penniless. The whole area was ashudder with violence and menace; it was difficult to know what to do for the best, and there was no one to give authoritative orders. But Tytler was a dedicated soldier and, considering what he had just lost, he badly needed to earn some money. So, when he was offered the job of paymaster with the British force that was being mustered to march back and recapture the capital, he accepted. As there was just no place for Harriet to find lodging in overcrowded Ambala, she decided to return with dear Robert as far as Delhi and then travel on alone to the nearest hill-station of Mussourie to await the birth of her child.

Thus it transpired that, much to her surprise, she found herself back with the assault forces in early June – and there was the Flagstaff Tower still standing, pocked with bullet holes and now being used as a battery-outpost by the British. The heat was excruciating; it reverberated off the sandstone rock in shimmering layers. Among the forces bivouacking in the burnt-out cantonments, mortality from sunstroke and 'heat apoplexy' was common – and from cholera, that illness 'that begins with death' and carried off two of the forces' Commanders-in-Chief within a month.

It was certainly no place for a woman in Harriet's condition, but when she and the few other wives who had accompanied their husbands were ordered to leave the field, a difficulty arose. The only transport that could be spared for the ladies were 'pad elephants' – so called because of the thick straw mattresses over their backs which riders had to clamber upon and cling to as best they might as the animals jogged along. But Harriet simply could not mount such a steed; it was a physical impossibility for her just then. 'Poor lady, poor lady, let her stay,' murmured the commanding officer to Robert when he heard of her plight. So she did, and thus became the only British woman on record to witness the entirety of the Delhi siege. On 21st June, thirty-six hours after the other ladies had left atop their elephants, Harriet, lying in an ammunition wagon with a thatch roof overhead, gave birth to a son. The event evoked one of the Mutiny's several well remembered lines: 'Now we'll be alright,' said an unknown private in Robert's regiment, 'we've had our first reinforcement.'

While the Tytlers were living through their ordeals at the Mutiny's first centre, the surge of rebellion spread over other parts of north India – along the valley of the Ganges, to Bareilly, Benares, Allahabad and Cawnpore. Cawnpore, most dire of all the names of 1857; already renowned in British annals ever since Emily Eden's day for an excess of dust and a deficiency of charm. The social life of its ten thousand or so Europeans was considered rather brash and brittle by those passing through from Delhi or Calcutta; its military personnel were said to be more than usually indolent and pleasure-seeking; the native town smelled worse than most because of the fetid canals and the stink of its tanneries where saddles, machine-belts and army boots were made; its surrounding districts had a bad reputation for thievery and violence. Here, in the words of W. Fitchett, a nineteenth-century historian, there took place in the summer of 1857 'a struggle in which Saxon courage and Hindu cruelty were exhibited in their highest measure, and which must always form one of the most heart-breaking and yet kindling traditions of the British race'. Such blatant bombast reads strangely now; but the reasons why that struggle roused so much passion and fury are still understandable, for it was at Cawnpore that one of the most revered of Victorian institutions, the English Lady, was slaughtered, defiled and brought low.

After the rapid fall of Delhi on 11th May, every British garrison in the north-west was on the alert; men slept with loaded guns at the ready; surreptitious plans for the evacuation of women and children were laid. But at nearly every station British soldiers were greatly outnumbered by sepoys, and so they had little choice but to stay put, hope for the best and pretend to trust the men they doubted. General Sir Hugh Wheeler, Commander-in-Chief at Cawnpore, was one of the oldest among the old school of Bengal officers and, like General Hewitt of Meerut, he could not believe that Mutiny would actually happen. 'All well at Cawnpore' he telegraphed Governor-General Lord Canning on 18th May.

Just in case things were not so well, he made provisional plans for the British to retreat to some half-built hospital barracks situated on the open plain outside the city. They were protected only by a small entrenchment and an earth wall, over which, it was later said, 'any cow could jump'. The city's well-stocked magazine he left in the hands of his sepoys, so as not to show any mistrust. Worse than that, Wheeler placed his trust in the Maharajah of Bithur, adopted son of Baji Rao, the last exiled leader of the Maratha Confederacy that had once challenged British power and lost. The Maharajah, popularly known among the British as the Nana Sahib, was a fat, jolly-seeming man of thirty-six years who lived in Birhur Palace just outside Cawnpore. During his exile, Baji Rao had enjoyed a substantial pension from the East India Company, but the Nana Sahib did not inherit it – a fact that greatly rankled. Yet he appeared to bear no grudge, and entertained the local Europeans now and then with lavish dinners and champagne picnics. Some of the guests sniggered at his western-style pretensions – a bedroom towel instead of a table napkin, a pudding served in a soup plate. But the Nana's larder was stuffed with goodies from Fortnum & Mason and there seemed no harm in him, even if he did have a rolling eye for the English ladies. So thought Wheeler, who asked the Nana's advice on methods of defence, and help in guarding the city treasury.

In spite of Wheeler's optimism, unrest, rumours and petty acts of insubordination accumulated in the ranks, and the townspeople refused to sell food to Europeans. Towards the end of May therefore, Wheeler ordered that all non-combatants should move into the barracks for safety. They did so – invalided soldiers, elderly civilians, women and children bringing their bundles of possessions and looking, wrote Amelia Horne, 'like so many travellers bound for a far country'. Amelia, one of the very few not bound, at that time, for the undiscovered bournes of that furthest of all countries, was a Eurasian girl, daughter of a deceased naval captain and Emma Cook, who was now married to the local agent for the North-West Dak Company in Cawnpore. She was a lively, pretty, resourceful eighteen-year-old, and so to her, though it was uncomfortable sleeping on the verandahs of the barracks with lots of others, it was also rather exciting, and she could not believe that anything worse would happen. Until it did, on the night of 4th June, when from the town there suddenly uprose the roars of men fighting, clatter of wheels and bayonets, crackle of weaponry and fire. Two days later a note from Nana Sahib arrived for Wheeler: 'I am about to attack you.'

It was a terrible blow to the British that their pet rajah had joined the mutineers; but whatever had been the extent of the Nana Sahib's duplicity in the past, he meant exactly what he said now. For the next twenty days the besieged British in the frail entrenchments suffered increasingly violent and concentrated attack from all sides by day and night. 'All the surrounding country was covered with men at arms,' Amelia wrote, as they were battered by a barrage from three mortars, two twenty-four pounders, three eighteen-pounders, two twelve-pounders and two nine-pounders, plus continuous volleys of musketry fire. Not that those on the receiving end knew or very much cared about such weight differentials, for every pound seemed like a ton of molten steel slung at them through the scorching air, every crack, whistle and thud was another herald of imminent pain and death. 'The bare recollection of the dreadful booming of the evening guns makes my heart sink even now,' wrote Amelia, when, as an old woman living in Calcutta, she recalled that nightmare.

She, her mother and sisters were cooped together with other women and children, and increasing numbers of wounded, in the one-storey barracks. Window-frames and doors were soon shot away, and shell-holes were blown in the brick-work. The roof of one barracks was 'pukka' built with cement, the other, used mainly as a shelter for the wounded and dying, was straw thatch. On the evening of 13th June, the latter caught fire, and, as Amelia wrote, the plight of its inmates 'confronted on one side by a burning building and on the other by shot and shell from the guns' was pitiful. Over forty of the besieged died that night, and from then on many of the non-combatants had no shelter whatsoever from the bombardments or from the sun which bore down on them at an average temperature of 120 degrees. The women, children and sick crouched together in the shallow trenches or behind the crumbled barrack walls; they were filthy, shattered in mind and body, hungry and gasping with thirst.

There were two wells in the encampment. Into one, at night,

were thrown the dead bodies that had swelled, smelled and festered on the ground all day; from the other water was drawn. Both were under such deadly continuous fire that many lives were lost in making desperate sorties to them. Amelia remembered the blackened tongues of the dying crying for water, and little children sucking the empty goat-skins for one drop of moisture. Sometimes the water they did get was tainted with blood or sewage. Food was almost as precious as water, and Amelia doled out sparse rations of parched gram (corn) and horseflesh soup to her little sisters. All medical supplies had been destroyed in the fire, and women tore up their skirts and petticoats for bandages. In the second week, Amelia's mother, who was seven months' pregnant, lost her reason and cowered, shrieking, in a ditch under the blazing sun. Amelia remembered her cries to her own dying day. 'Great God was it possible that human beings could endure so much?' she asked herself.

The fatalities from wounds, sunstroke, fevers and dementia increased daily. 'There were those who endured in one day a double or treble bereavement,' wrote G. Trevelyan, the siege's most colourful chronicler, 'while in some families none remained to mourn.' Those who did sometimes envied the dead, and yet the flickering hope of eventual rescue kept them alive. But no rescue came. Messages describing their extremity had been smuggled out, and a relief force under Brigadier Havelock had been mustered in Calcutta, for the relief of Cawnpore and the other besieged garrison at Lucknow. But its supplies of weapons and transport were so insufficient that the men could not push rapidly enough through the six hundred miles of the Ganges Valley area that was in a state of violent uprising. By the third week of the siege, the Cawnpore garrison, who knew little of the troubled conditions elsewhere, felt themselves abandoned by the world. 'Surely we are not to be left to die like rats in a cage?' read one of Wheeler's last messages to Sir Henry Lawrence, who was in charge of the forces defending Lucknow.

Faced with that prospect, people clutch at any straw. On 25th June a woman holding a white handkerchief approached the battered entrenchments bringing a message to Wheeler from the

Nana Sahib. It promised 'a safe passage to Allahabad' for all survivors who were 'in no way connected with the acts of Lord Dalhousie and are willing to lay down their arms'. Tense negotiations followed; the British leaders hated the very word surrender and some of them did not trust the Nana. The women, with less thought of honour, more for the lives of their remaining children, prayed silently for deliverance. The next day their prayers seemed answered – the Nana conceded to the British request for an 'honourable' surrender that would allow them to march with hand-arms from the entrenchments to boats that would carry them down to Allahabad.

It was a 'great day', Amelia remembered. The besieged, with returning appetite for life, finished most of the provisions; the able-bodied soldiers drummed march tunes on old casks to cheer everyone up. The children, skinny, sun-blistered and boil-covered, watched the preparations for departure silently, as did the women, some of whom, said Amelia, looked 'old, haggard, desperate and imbecile'. But still alive – after all they had endured in the past three weeks, surely they deserved to live now?

At dawn on the 27th, the pathetic remnant of the Cawnpore garrison straggled out of that foul place on the barren plain as from a prison camp, reduced – as all can be reduced by the long suffering of pain, terror and deprivation – to wretched, diseased and filthy skeletons, loathsome to the eyes of other humankind. The hostile eyes of the sepoys and townspeople watched them passing, some in dhoolies or bullock-carts, a few on elephants provided by the Nana Sahib, others on foot carrying bundles of clothes or babies. On the banks of the Ganges, flat boats with thatch awnings were moored. The embarkation took a long time for no native came forward to help aboard the sick, the pregnant or the young. The river glinted a promise of escape in the morning sun; the swords and muskets of the watchful sepoys also glinted. There was a sinister hush, broken only by the occasional groans and cries of the afflicted and the frightened. Amelia clawed her way aboard one boat with her stepfather and sisters, and huddled under the awning, praying to be floated away on the bright water from this dreadful place.

Suddenly a bugle blasted the silence and at the sound all the native rowers on the boats jumped into the water and made for the shore; then the sepoys' rifles cracked into action and simultaneously the boat-roofs, ignited by charcoal embers secreted by the boatmen, burst into flames. Realizing the extent of the betrayal, the British returned the fire. But the place was a death-trap. The boats could not be moved, the guns raked their decks and the water on all sides. People floundered into the water, wounded and drowning; they were burnt or bayoneted to death by sepoys who waded after them on horseback. Very soon, says Trevelyan, 'the dead outnumbered the living'.

From that first massacre only four men escaped in one of the boats to tell, eventually, the terrible tale. But some of the women and children were, it seemed, to be spared. About a hundred and twenty-five of them were dragged ashore by the sepoys in a state of utter wretchedness and despair – what further tortures could be in store? They were herded from the riverbank and enclosed in a small building called the Bibighur – the Ladies' House, once the dwelling of the Indian mistress of a British officer. For eighteen days they were incarcerated in conditions so dreadful that eighteen of the women and seven children died. On the evening of 15th July, by which time the relieving force under Havelock was at last approaching the city, the prisoners inside the Bibighur were stabbed, clubbed and hacked to death by five butchers summoned from the local bazaar to perform a task which even the sepoys refused to undertake. The next morning, the dead, and a few, alas, still just alive, were dragged out of that slaughterhouse and thrown into a nearby well.

And Amelia Horne? When the massacre in the river began, she watched the other members of her family being slashed, burnt or drowned and was herself thrown into the water by a sepoy. At the last moment she was hauled out of the river by an Indian trooper who, in the general confusion, managed to carry her off on his horse and hide her in a nearby shed. Later she was clothed in Mohammedan female dress and carried to two priests, who stood over her with drawn swords while they intoned the service of her 'conversion' to the faith. Following the ceremony, the trooper took her as his wife and forced her to accompany him on his various campaigns. Eventually, after a series of harrowing and extremely unpleasant experiences, she escaped, and thus became the only woman known to survive the Cawnpore siege.

Two days after its final bloody act, men of the 84th and 78th Highland Regiments reached the city. They forced open the door of the Ladies' House; they peered down that dire well. All the signs of slaughter still pulsed in the hot sun; in the well, mutilated limbs festered. The soldiers vomited, fainted, cursed the heavens in their rage. What they saw in that room of death – scraps of children's clothes and toys, fragments of letters, bloodsoaked prayer-books, broken combs and locks of severed hair – brought out all that was most vengeful and cruel in them. They went on a rampage of savage and promiscuous retribution through the city over which most of the historians of the time drew a reticent veil. Brigadier-General James Neill issued an order that every captured rebel should be forced to clean a portion of the blood-stained house by licking it with his tongue before his execution. It was a return to the most primitive kind of barbaric warfare, and it probably would not have been permitted had Brigadier Havelock retained the Cawnpore command. But, during the third week of July, Havelock, dreading that he might again be too late to avert total disaster, marshalled a contingent of his men and pushed on hastily towards the north-east – and the city of Lucknow.

Chapter Eight

Henry Lawrence, who, since the death of his wife three years before, had looked and sometimes felt like the 'old man' he was often affectionately termed by his younger admirers, was dying in a house belonging to one Dr Joseph Fayrer, which stood in the besieged compound of the Residency at Lucknow in the province of Oudh. On the morning of 2nd July, only a few days after the siege began, Henry's groin was shattered by a shell from an enemy howitzer as he lay resting. The news of his approaching demise caused general consternation and sorrow, for, since the end of May, when the first signs of impending mutiny appeared in the city, Henry had been the driving force of inspiration and leadership to the entire garrison.

He had been appointed Chief Commissioner of Oudh that March, an assignment which, though an honour, had filled him with misgivings from the outset. For Oudh had been annexed by the British in the previous year – an aggressive act that caused a great deal of discontent and hostility among its inhabitants and in the Bengal Army, many of whose sepoys were recruited from that province. Henry, with his ear close to the native ground, guessed that there was trouble in store, and, since his arrival, had pursued a policy of conciliation and reform designed to quell the growing unrest. He had been one of the few to warn the government of the possibility of open mutiny. 'We measure too much by English rule,' he had written to Lord Canning, and urged that the natives, especially the sepoys, should be treated 'as having much the same feelings, the same ambition, the same perception of ability and imbecility as ourselves'. In fact there was a distinct lack of perception and ability among the government leaders at that time, and Henry, his words disregarded, set about doing what he could to strengthen the British position in the province. His wholehearted dedication was an inspiration to many: 'He had done with the world except working for it while his strength lasted,' wrote Herbert Edwardes. 'He had come to that calm, peaceful estimate of time and eternity, of himself and the judgements which could only come of wanting and finding Christ.'

During late May and June, when the rebel attacks were concentrated on Delhi and Cawnpore, Henry, who had full military and civil responsibility for the Residency defence, gave orders for fortifications to be built. On the perimeters of the Residency – a term used to describe the building itself and the whole area in which it stood – lines of defence were defined with palisades, trenches, sand-bagged batteries, and within and beneath the several buildings in the compound, arms, treasure and sufficient provisions to feed hundreds for several months were stored. 'The peril of mutiny was certain,' wrote W. Fitchett, whose *Tale of the Great Mutiny* is written in the grand, proud, nineteenth-century style, 'but was uncertain in scale, and time and form.' Henry Lawrence, overtly cheerful and indefatigable, was secretly preparing for the worst, and this was as well, for the ordeal of Lucknow was to be long and harsh.

When, at the end of June, the 'siege proper' began, there were living within the Residency about three thousand people; about seventeen hundred of these were fighting men (including seven hundred Indian soldiers who 'remained true to their salt', as the British put it,) and about six hundred were English and Eurasian women and children. It was estimated that the besiegers numbered between eight to ten thousand, heavily outnumbering the British. The non-combatants were given billets in the largest private houses away from the perimeters – in the Residency, and homes belonging to Mr Gubbins, the Financial Commissioner, and Dr Fayrer; others found themselves in the Begum Kothi, a collection of small buildings and courtyards where native ladies of the King of Oudh's court had once lived.

The most comfortable quarters were naturally in the Residency itself and were occupied by wives of the leading officers, among them Julia Inglis, wife of Brigadier John Inglis, and Mrs Adelaide Case. On 30th June, Adelaide's husband, Colonel William Case, had taken part in the last sortie made outside the Residency. An expeditionary force of about seven hundred men had attacked the mutineers in a village near Lucknow and been disastrously defeated; more than two hundred, including William Case, were killed. The garrison was still reeling from that defeat when Sir Henry was shot. 'We were indeed grieved,' wrote Julia Inglis, 'for independently of the loss he would be, we all loved as a friend the dear old man who seemed to live only to do good.'

He lived forty-eight hours longer in extreme agony, able in lucid moments to give detailed instructions to Major Banks (his civilian successor) and John Inglis (who took over military command), about the future conduct of the siege, and to murmur recollections of his children and his beloved wife. He died on 4th July in his fifty-first year. They took from his neck the locket with Honoria's picture in it that he had always worn, and buried him without any fuss, as he had wished, in a trench with five other soldiers who had fallen that day.

From then on the situation in the Residency deteriorated for everybody. The enemy fire was continuous and heavy, day and night: 'To give you an idea how incessant it was,' wrote Adelaide Case's cousin, Caroline, afterwards, 'I must tell you that when it ceased we quite missed it and felt almost uncomfortable.' Caroline, Adelaide, and Julia Inglis were living in a small whitewashed room furnished with two sofas, sleeping mats and with the luxury of an adjoining bathroom (half filled with grain for their three goats). They also enjoyed the services of Mrs Inglis' four servants who had 'remained loyal'. All in all, they were, as they knew, luckier than most. 'Many of our ladies were put to sore straits as the siege continued,' Julia wrote. 'They had no servants and had to cook their own food and wash their own clothes. Firewood was scarce, owing to the principal stock being turned into a rampart; and I have seen ladies going out at the risk of being shot to pick up sticks. The palings of the Residency Garden disappeared in this way.'

One of the ladies whose straits became sorer was Maria Germon, wife of Lieutenant Charles Germon, her 'dear old Charlie', of the 13th Bengal Native Infantry. Maria was quartered in the home of Dr and Mrs Fayrer, in whose drawing-room Henry Lawrence died. On the day before his death, all the servants, fearing the worst, decamped, 'so we were obliged to do everything – even wash up plates and dishes etc. and perhaps it was a good thing, it kept our thoughts from dwelling on our misery,' Maria decided.

Indeed, for her and for most of the other women, the siege experience consisted largely of endless, unaccustomed chores which had to be carried out in filthy, crowded, hot rooms with no sanitation, and were beset by misery, sickness and the danger of sudden, violent death. Maria's journal for July is a macabre litany of the last, recorded with that strange acceptance of the formerly incredible which conditions of catastrophe produce. 'Poor Captain Frances this night had one leg taken off and the other shattered by a round shot while sitting on top of the Brigade Mess.' While she was making teas two days later, 'an order came down for hot water bottles, Mr Dashwood being taken with cholera . . . About twelve Mr Harris administered the Sacrament to him and about one o'clock he died.' Mr Harris' clerical colleague, Mr Pole-hampton, 'was hit in the body by a musket-shot' and died twelve days later. Mr Harris reckoned himself fortunate when, after a quiet day, he 'had only one funeral this evening'.

And yet, through all this, one simply had to keep going, as Maria did. On Saturday, 18th July she wrote an account of her daily routine, its heroics verging on the mundane: 'Rose a little before six and made tea for all the party – seventeen . . . Then, with Mrs Anderson, gave out attah, rice, sugar, sago etc. for the day's ration. While doing it a 6-lb. shot came through the verandah above, broke down some plates and bricks and fell at our feet . . . I then rushed to the bheestie who was passing and made him fill a tin can with water which I lugged upstairs, then bathed and dressed. It was about half-past eight when I was ready, so I went to the front door to get a breath of fresh air. At nine, down again to make tea again for breakfast, which consisted of roast mutton, chappattis, rice and jam . . .'

The women's world was, perforce, thus constricted. Outside, in the thick of the action, the men repulsed a variety of attacks – the mutineers dug tunnels for mines under the Residency defence-lines, they attempted to clamber silently over the retaining walls at night, they stormed the vulnerable outer batteries repeatedly. Subjected to all this, the lists of killed and wounded lengthened, and living conditions within the garrison worsened. In late July, Brigadier Inglis' aide-de-camp noted that 'Commissariat returns were lessened every third day so as to eke out our resources . . . Bad smells from imperfectly buried bodies were horrible, the want of a change of diet was beginning to be felt, and in addition to other disease, cholera, smallpox and especially scurvy began to be fearfully prevalent . . . Scurvy took the form of loose teeth, swollen heads and boils, and gained the name of "garrison disease".'

The hands of Katherine Bartrum were covered with boils, but 'my fingers must work away notwithstanding their being so painful', she wrote. For Katherine had to feed and wash her little baby Bobbie, and then sit beside him and fan the flies and mosquitoes from his pale face, because he was so ill and frail; and she had to collect wood to heat his daily ration of goat's milk which, in these strange times, was 'more precious than gold'. Katherine was twenty-three years old, the daughter of a silversmith of Bath, and her slender book, *Reminiscences of Lucknow* is the most touching and vivid of several written by besieged ladies.

Her predicament was worse than most because she had been forced to flee at the eleventh hour to Lucknow from Gonda, about eighty miles away, and thus had had no chance to accumulate any little extra comforts which eased the lot of those who were already resident in the city. At Gonda, she and her young doctor husband, Robert, had been 'living for the past eight months the peaceful and retired life of an officer's family in an up-country station' – until it was shattered by the news of the outbreaks at Meerut and Delhi. 'I cannot describe to you what our feelings have been lately,' she wrote to her father in England at the end of May. 'Only ten Europeans in the place, completely at the mercy of the natives. What could we do if they chose to rise?'

Plans for fortifying the Bartrum house were considered, and

then came talk of 'sending Mrs Clark and myself with our children down the river in a native boat to Calcutta, which we strongly opposed; for it would be better to die with our husbands than leave them alone.' But the tales of 'bloodshed and horror' worsened with every mail, every rumour that filtered to their vulnerable little outpost. By 6th June, 'the Police Sowars show symptoms of rising. The Clarks sleep at our bungalow. Unquiet nights and weary days; all things are insecure.' She kept a sword under her pillow and 'dear Robert had his pistol loaded ready'.

Then came orders from Lucknow that all women and children in the small stations were to proceed at once to the city for safety and – oh the agony of that! 'Often had I contemplated death with my husband, but not separation from him . . . Most earnestly did I plead that I might be allowed to remain with him, but he convinced me that, were it only for my baby's sake, I ought to go into Lucknow.' Heavy-hearted, she hastily packed a few things for the baby, and then the Bartrums and the Clarks rode sixteen miles together as far as Secrora, where the men had to say farewell and return to their post. 'They put us on our elephants, and well do I remember Robert's cheerful, "Good-bye dear Kate, keep up your spirits. We shall soon meet again, and take care of my little darling."

She tried very hard to do his bidding through the anxious vicissitudes that followed. First the terrors of that late-night elephant-ride, accompanied by armed men whom she and Mrs Clark could not trust; then the arrival at the Residency and into a scene of the 'utmost confusion', where she knew no one and was allotted a lowly billet in the Begum Kothi, 'a most uninviting place, so dirty, having neither a punkah to cool the air or a scrap of furniture to set it off, but we had to make the best of it'. Fifteen women and children in one room that first night making the best of it, and with no real air to breathe between them.

Katherine undertook most of the cleaning and tidying chores, 'for most of my fellow sufferers are too ill, mentally and bodily, to care how things look'. In the evenings, when the children were asleep, the women gathered round 'a chair which formed our tea table, sitting on the bedside and drinking tea (not the strongest in the world) by the light of a candle which was stuck in a bottle . . . and then we talked together of bygone days, of happy homes in England where our childhood had been spent'. And before going to rest they prayed, oh, so fervently, for the survival of their ailing children, and their husbands who were fleeing or fighting or dying somewhere in the dark menacing land that India had become.

Then death closed in on them too. Mrs Hale with cholera was the first to die in the Begum Kothi; then Mrs Thompson with smallpox; then Mrs Clark, Katherine's friend from Gonda, was confined and sank gradually, her baby with her. She asked Katherine to pack her boxes, 'as she was going on a long journey and must have everything prepared. I did what she wished, sorted her things and put them in the boxes. "Thank you," she said, "the dhoolie is here, but the bearers have not come . . ." I gave her arrowroot and from that time she never spoke again.' And then Bobbie contracted cholera and nearly died, and Katherine herself was taken ill and was 'almost too weak to hold him. There was no kind husband near to cheer and comfort me at this trying time, and my chief anxiety was about my babe, for if I should be taken away, who would there be to care for him?'

Certainly the most fortunate women were those with husbands near at hand, for it was a time when family considerations took priority. Luckily for Maria Germon, her 'dear old Charlie' bore a charmed life; even though he was stationed at one of the most exposed posts and, during one attack, 'a bullet entered his helmet at the side and went out at the top, carrying the ventilator with it'. Indestructible, he popped in to see her every day and each time her 'heart was gladdened' with the relief of his coming. He brought her little treats – a tin of soup, a tough biscuit, and once a whole bottle of port; one never asked where such goodies came from. In return, Maria tried to keep his uniforms mended and clean, for, like everyone else, he was showing signs of wear and tear, and there was a brisk trade in the clothes of the dead. A servant hawked round a box containing four smart bonnets one day and had three offers for them; Maria used a piece of Mr Harris' habit to mend 'Charlie's unmentionables', and bought herself a silk dress which, in optimistic moments, she planned to wear when the siege was raised.

But when, oh when, would that be? In late July came rumours that the relief force under General Havelock was at hand, but the news proved premature, and in the after-wash of hope deferred, a weary, melancholy sense of abandonment and defeat swamped them all. Maria Germon wrote: 'We feel now like a ship becalmed. The future is a perfect blank. We are not able to give even a surmise of what our fate will be – but we have all made up our minds never to give in, but to blow up all in the entrenchments sooner.' In the anxious night hours when the musketry rattled and the shells pounded, the women in the dim, rat-infested rooms underground discussed the eventuality of final defeat. Some kept laudanum or prussic acid to hand, some made suicide pacts with their husbands; others, like Adelaide Case, felt such means could not be right. 'All we have to do is . . . to be prepared for our death and leave the rest in the hands of Him who knows what is best for us,' was her conclusion.

In the meantime life had to be sustained. Food supplies were decreasing; the Commissariat claimed three of Mrs Inglis' goats; she carefully weighed out all supplies for her house every morning, with a little extra arrowroot or sugar for the sick children; in the Begum Kothi they had run out of candles, and burned cotton-wicks in oil. On 27th August Henry Lawrence's stores were sold – a ham went for fifty rupees and twenty bottles of sherry for a hundred and ten. 'People bid recklessly,' Maria noted, 'running up bills which they didn't expect to live long enough to pay.' The Germons however had a robust faith in survival, and Charlie bought nothing but 'a pair of soldier's high-lows for eight rupees. – More useful than truffled larks.' But the very next day more bad news was smuggled through which seemed to confirm the fears of the reckless. The message was from General Havelock saying that it would be about another three weeks before he could even attempt their relief – three weeks; an eternity. 'All is over with us; we can't hold out till then,' was Julia Inglis' first cry when she heard the news.

A principal reason for the delay was that, in the national context of the Mutiny, Delhi had to be recaptured first, and only then would there be sufficient troops to reinforce the numbers arriving from England and Hongkong for the march on Lucknow. For, during that whole violent summer, the Delhi Force had sweltered, sworn and suffered on the rocky sandstone Ridge overlooking the capital. The temperature sometimes rose to 131 degrees in the 'shade' of the tents; outside there was no shade at all.

Very soon after the birth of its youngest recruit, the Force had been more substantially buttressed by the arrival of Sikhs, Gurkhas and Afghan cavalry from John Lawrence's Punjab Frontier Force. Tents mushroomed along the Ridge, supply-lines lengthened, a dirty, busy little settlement of food bazaars, stables, huts for camp-followers grew up outside the big city, inside which thousands of sepoys congregated. The mutineers attacked repeatedly, trying to dislodge the British from their commanding position, and the British repulsed repeatedly. 'Week after week the fighting went on most gallantly,' Fitchett wrote. 'And the story gleams with records of shining pluck; it rings with the clash of steel on steel; it thrills to the rattle of musketry volleys and the deeper voice of the cannon.'

For Harriet Tytler there was not much of the ringing thrill about it. Seeking greater safety, she had moved into a bell-of-arms, a small circular stone tower with one door and no windows, normally used as a weapon store. There, with her faithful French maid and the children, she tried to recover her strength, resting on a straw-covered floor. Rains came and the roof leaked, wetting all their quilts; when the sun returned it was like being roasted in a grubby little oven. But outside the bell-of-arms it was much worse. Cholera swept through the camp felling men like ninepins as they stood on picket duty. This was not surprising, for the garrison's kitchens were situated next to the cesspits, and the canal water they had to drink was as turgid as pea soup; Harriet had to hold her nose and close her eyes to gulp it down. Flies pullulated on the messes of faeces, vomit and half-buried corpses in the cemetery near the bell-of-arms. During one engagement Harriet reckoned that a hundred bullets hit the tower, several whistling through the two holes which Robert had knocked in the wall to provide a little air. 'We never knew from day to day whether we should live to see the close of it,' Harriet wrote. But they continued to survive. Frank, the eldest child, played soldiers round the tents and was everybody's mascot; the new baby, born into the cacophony of war, slept peacefully through every shelling.

In early August, John Nicholson, the most flamboyant and singular of all Henry Lawrence's young men, reached the Ridge after a series of gruelling forced marches from the Punjab, and took command of the faltering force with the brilliant mastery of purpose that was characteristic of his short, strange life. By the month's end there were 8,748 fighting men poised on the Ridge ready to attack and on 7th September their every battery 'broke into wrathful thunder on the city', Fitchett wrote.

In a fortnight of grim fighting during which well over three thousand British and Indian soldiers were killed – among them Nicholson in a typically daredevil frontal charge on the Lahore Gate – Delhi was recaptured. The firing, which had gone on almost continuously for three and a half months, ceased and the comparative silence that fell was, Harriet wrote, 'somehow strange and indescribably sad'. By the time she, the one memsahib to have experienced the entire siege, was allowed to re-enter Delhi in the company of her husband, it 'looked like a city of the dead' – empty blasted houses, old women and children cowering in alleyways, only a few cats bold or hungry enough to come sniffing round them. The fall of the capital, the subsequent capture of the old King and the execution of the royal princes was the turning point of the Mutiny; from then on the ultimate restoration of British rule was inevitable. But there were still lives to be gambled and lost, still battles to be fought, and the most dramatic of these, the final full-scale set-piece, was the Relief of Lucknow.

By mid-September, when the battle for possession of Delhi was in progress, the besieged in the Residency had come almost to take for granted the incredibility of their predicament on the one hand and the tenacity of their survival powers on the other. 'If this ever reaches my dear ones at home,' wrote Maria Germon in her journal, 'they will wonder when I tell them that my bed is not fifty yards from the eighteen-pounder in our compound – only one room between us, and yet I lie as quietly when it goes off without shutting my ears as if I had been used to it all my life. Eighty days of siege life does wonders.'

After eighty days of the same relentless sounds – guns, shells, the various cries of human distress – Adelaide Case would coolly risk a stray bullet every sunset to creep into the nearest courtyard to hear the cooing of some captive doves. Eighty days of living on 'basics' had so up-ended all previous definitions of value that it no longer seemed incredible to hear of a handful of precious jewels, looted from the treasury, being exchanged for one bottle of brandy, and, as Maria said, a quarter pound of sugar begged from the Commissariat and shared among the ladies of Dr Fayrer's house 'made twenty people as merry as formerly a dinner with the Governor-General would have done'. Eighty days without proper washing facilities, nutritious food or adequate fresh air intensified the miseries and sufferings of the non-combatants. 'A discovery made of Light Infantry (lice) in a lady's head,' wrote Maria in horror on 11th September. Five days later it was discovered that 'only two ladies of the garrison found free of Light Infantry'. Maria, who suggests she was one of the fortunate, made a close-fitting cap to guard against contamination, for fifteen ladies' heads lay under the same punkah every night.

The young suffered most, and, on the same day that two enemy mines were discovered in underground tunnels near the Residency house and harmlessly detonated, Maria noted that Mrs Boileau's baby was seriously ill. Elizabeth, wife of Colonel George Boileau, had fled to Lucknow from Secrora just ahead of Katherine Bartrum, but, having friends in higher places than the junior doctor's wife, she had secured a place for herself and her children in Dr Fayrer's house. As the weeks went by she watched helplessly as her baby daughter grew ever paler and more feeble. Sores and rashes appeared all over her body and her throat became so ulcerated that she could not swallow. Elizabeth sat for days and nights holding the infant in her lap and thinking 'Oh how shall I bear to lose her . . . Oh my pet lamb is going from me . . .' On 9th September, the child seemed to rally and 'sat up and talked and laughed in her own old pretty way'. But the doctor shook his head and told Mrs Boileau not to hope. On the 13th, 'after such a night of agony and painful watching I pray God I may never spend again', the baby died. 'Sergeant Court has made a little coffin and ere long my pretty Babe must take her place among the hundreds in that wretched mournful churchyard,' Elizabeth wrote. 'Oh God Almighty comfort me . . . Oh dear, I am weary . . . weary . . .'

At the end of eighty days they were all weary indeed. The monsoon rains came, washing away some of the frailer defence works, pouring through the damaged ceiling of Mrs Inglis' room in the Residency until the floor was like a lake. On 18th September there was a partial eclipse of the sun and the remaining native servants foretold fresh disasters; the next day, Maria Germon, feeling 'very poorly', took to her bed and Charlie managed to scrounge a bottle of port wine for her. She was still in bed three days later when the splendid news for which they had all prayed so long came. It was contained in a smuggled letter written by Sir James Outram, joint commander with Havelock, and began: 'The army crossed the river yesterday – and all the material being over now, marches towards you tomorrow, and under the blessing of God will now relieve you.'

Next day the firing of the Relief Force guns was heard by the besieged and 'the smoke of the guns seen from the top of the Residency – oh joy!' recorded Maria, the hope of release making her feel very much better. Advancing on Lucknow, the British had to cut their way through every street of the city; at last, as Fitchett put it, 'from the head of the column rose a mighty shout. It was not the cry of soldiers at the charge full of the wrath of battle. It was a great cry of exaltation and triumph. Through the grey twilight, dark with eddying smoke, the leading files of the British had seen the battered archway of the Bailey Guard. The goal was reached.'

Inside the Residency everyone was tense with excitement. 'About 5 p.m.' wrote Maria, 'we heard cheering, and immediately saw the troops rushing in – the 78th Highlanders foremost, and our house being the first, our compound was instantly filled and the officer heading the Highlanders rushed up and shook hands with us ladies all round, and then threw himself into a chair, quite exhausted ... It was the most exciting scene I ever witnessed – The Piper sprang on a chair and he and Mrs Anderson claimed acquaintance – he asked her where she came from – she said, Edinburgh, and he answered, So do I, and from the Castle Hill. Then they shook hands and he sent round the word that there was a lady from Edinburgh and then gave another turn on his bagpipes.'

The scene later crystallized into one of the set-pieces of the British Imperial Story in India: the brawny Highlanders triumphantly scooping up and kissing the siege-wan children, the Lucknow ladies gazing up with brimful eyes and arms outstretched in gratitude towards their deliverers; the gruff commanders vigorously shaking hands with each other, almost too overcome to speak. And, for backdrop, the smoke of the cannon, the battered gates, the wounded begging for water and the sheer muddle of it all – camels and horses and foot soldiers and bearers, kitbags and bedding-rolls, baggage- and bullock-carts and people searching desperately for familiar faces and clamouring for news.

'The noise, confusion and cheering were almost overwhelming,' wrote Katherine Bartrum. 'My first thought was of my husband, whether he had accompanied the reinforcement. And I was not long left in suspense, for the first officer I spoke to told me he was come up with them and they had shared the same dhoolie the previous night.' She ran out, carrying her baby dressed in his best, to see if she could find him, 'watching the face of everyone that came in the Bailey Gate'. But he was not there and she heard that he was with the heavy artillery and would arrive on the morrow. So she went back to the hateful little room in the Begum Kothi and put Bobbie to bed and longed for the morning.

All the next day she waited for Robert, carrying her baby around the courtyards and up to the Residency roof and looking hopefully down along the confused streets outside. The next day she was still waiting, suddenly aware that people were avoiding her anxious eyes, and her heart grew sick with foreboding. 'This afternoon Dr. Darby came to me. He looked so kindly and sadly in my face, and I said to him, "How strange it is my husband's not come in". "Yes", he said, "it is strange", and turned round and went out of the room.' That evening they sent another widow, Mrs

Polehampton who 'had passed through the furnace herself', to tell Katherine that Robert had been killed at the very gates of the Residency. They brought her his fine black horse, his sword and instrument case. She clasped her child to her bosom and screamed and cared little any more about the progress of the siege.

Few of the ladies had to endure such a dramatic fall from hope to bitterest dispair, but the euphoria engendered by the arrival of Havelock's force was short-lived for everybody. On the 27th, the day Katherine was told of her husband's death, another woman, Adelaide Case, one of the earliest bereft, wrote in her journal, 'After all this has been a very painful day, everyone is depressed and all feel that we are in fact not relieved.' They were not – only reinforced. Havelock's force had been too small in the first place and had sustained such fearful losses in reaching the Residency that it could not break out again – especially as it was now encumbered with well over a thousand non-combatants, women, children and wounded. Moreover, the men who had come in brought very few provisions for themselves, but plenty of bad news for the besieged who, for the first time, heard the full details of the Cawnpore massacre and the Delhi siege. 'It was impossible to realize such horrors,' wrote Julia Inglis, 'and to hear them made one's very heart sick.'

It made the hearts of the women sick too when the noise of battle was renewed, even redoubled, as the Lucknow defenders, now under the command of Sir James Outram, made sorties to extend their perimeters and try to force a safe passage out through the city. As the rebels had been driven back from the immediate vicinity of the Residency area, it was safer for the women to move around the compound, and Maria Germon was 'perfectly thunder-struck' to see dear Charlie's garrison building, 'such a mass of ruins, not a part on either side of it that is not riddled with round shot and bullets'. She sat on a box in one room with him and had a cup of tea, 'of course without milk or sugar, but it seemed Paradise to be alone with him again'. But the happy interlude was brief, for it seemed that, after all the excitement and optimism of the breakthrough, the siege was going on just as before and 'there seems to be a perfect stagnation of everything', Adelaide Case decided.

Indeed in some ways conditions were worse, for there was now a total of 6,938 mouths to feed – 2,866 of them European, 755 Indian troops and 3,317 camp-followers and servants. Capable Marie Germon was made mistress of the provisions in Dr Fayrer's house and doled out reduced rations each day – twelve ounces of very tough bullock meat for a man, six of the same for a woman, two for a child, together with unsifted flour for chappattis, rice and salt. One Sunday, for a special treat, Dr Fayrer shot sufficient sparrows to make a 'sparrow curry', but Maria herself 'could not be induced to taste it'. On 2nd October Julia Inglis noted that, for the very first time since the siege began, she had appetite for more food than was allowed her, and any 'extra piece of chappatti was a great treat for us all'.

Things were harsher, as usual, in the other billets where the ladies had to wage constant war against rats and insects to preserve what stores they had. In the soap-less and candle-less Begum Kothi they ground dhal between stones and made a paste of it to wash clothes, 'But we have so little that it is a question of whether we shall use it to wash with or to eat,' Katherine Bartrum wrote. In the blankness of her misery she cared little either way, the days running together, for 'all looks so dark and there is no sweet hope now of meeting my husband whenever relief may come'. She lived only for Bobbie, who seemed to be growing stronger, though he 'has such an old, sad look'. His sole amusement was calling to the monkeys that played around the courtyards; others of the besieged looked at them more speculatively – wondering if they would soon be reduced to eating horse-stew and monkey-pie.

For the relatively fortunate Germons, the continuance of the siege was uncomfortable, fatiguing but scarcely unendurable. In spite of the dangers from round shot and snipers' bullets within the compound area, the ladies started calling on each other's quarters to compare hardships, and Maria used often to run over and see Charlie at his outpost for a cosy chat and tea. At last, in early November, they learned of the approach of the second major relief force, under Sir Colin Campbell, and Charlie helped to rig up the semaphore on the Residency roof which was to renew contact with the small reserve force that had been left behind in the royal park of Alambagh outside the city when the main detachment had broken through to the Residency. Soon the Lucknow commanders learned from smuggled messages that two hundred and fifty more support troops had gained the Alambagh and contingents of British were moving steadily up-country and massing for the relief.

It was just a matter of time now and rather anti-climactic after the grand excitement of the first 'relief'. The ladies got quite upset at the thought of actually moving again, and palkis, buggy-carts and bearers were suddenly much in demand. Mrs Inglis was anxious to find a servant from among the widowed soldiers' wives to accompany her to England. Charlie and Maria spent 12th November 'arranging and packing our worldly goods' in preparation for a speedy withdrawal from the Residency. That evening they heard that Sir Colin Campbell had reached the Alambagh with five thousand men under his command. His force comprised Highlanders, bold Sikh horsemen in long riding boots and red turbans, two regiments of Native Infantry from the Punjab, a Naval Brigade from Hongkong, troops of the Bengal Infantry and Artillery, some of whom had survived the Ridge at Delhi and looked down the well at Cawnpore.

Riding in review of his troops on the day before the battle, Sir Colin had stopped at the lines of the 93rd Highlanders and, says Fitchett, 'Campbell's Celtic blood kindled' at the sight of them – the kilts and the pipes, the bonnet-plumes tossing in the wind. '"Ninety-third," he said, "you are my own lads; I rely on you to do the work." And a voice from the ranks in broadest Doric answered, "Ay, ay, Sir Colin, ye ken us and we ken you. We'll bring the women and children out of Lucknow or die wi' ye in the attempt."' So the British stormed into the battered capital of the province of Oudh once again, and this time did succeed in rescuing the women and children, though over five hundred men died in the accomplishment of it. Maria Germon, peeping through a hole in the parapet of Charlie's outpost, 'saw the mines spring and the batteries firing furiously . . . A most extraordinary scene'. And she could see in the distance the 'peculiar caps' of the Lancers as they advanced along the Motee Mohul road and, near at hand, a few harassed, hapless natives trying to escape from it all by swimming across the River Gumti with bundles of clothes tied on their heads.

The Residency was officially relieved on 17th November and orders were issued for the complete withdrawal of all personnel, for Campbell had decided to evacuate the long-beleaguered and much-weakened garrison first. It was a sensible decision, for there were an estimated four thousand mutineers in the vicinity of Lucknow and it would need a much larger force to resist them and recapture the city itself. So, with a strange sense of reluctance and unreality, the Lucknow ladies packed up their plate, linen and a few prized possessions – but 'all our glass and crockery we were obliged to leave behind us', Adelaide Case said regretfully. Katherine Bartrum had no choice but to travel light: 'Well, I can only carry my baby and my worldly effects can be put into a very small compass since they consist merely of a few old clothes.'

Maria, having survived without any drastic losses so far, was not going to risk deprivation at this late juncture. Charlie, who had a knack of getting hold of the right thing at the right time, managed to hire a pony for her to ride and a servant to carry her boxes. On the day of the withdrawal of the non-combatants, which was to be carried out as secretly as possible, she dressed in all, but *all*, her clothes: 'Four flannel waistcoats, three pairs of stockings, three chemises, three drawers, one flannel and four white petticoats, my pink flannel dressing-gown, skirt, plaid jacket and over all my loose dress and jacket that I had made out of my habit – then tied my cashmere shawl sash-fashion round my waist, and also Charlie's silver mug and put on a worsted cap and hat, and had my drab cloak put on the saddle. I forgot to say I had sewed dear mother's fish knife and fork in my pink skirt, and had put a lot of things in the pocket of it. I had also two under-pockets, one filled with jewellery and a card-case, the other with my journal and valuable papers. I then filled my cloth skirt pocket with pencil, knife, pin-cushion, handkerchief etc. All my lace was sewn up in a bag which I wore also.' It cost Charlie and his chum, Captain Weston, a great deal of exertion to get her up on the pony 'which was no joke dressed and laden as I was and with no spring in me.' Joke or not, 'Captain Weston and a large party were in fits of laughter . . .'

And so, after a hundred and forty days, the ladies of Lucknow left the Residency in the gathering twilight, with an escort of fifteen hundred men to see them safely through the still turbulent city. Of the six hundred women who had suffered the siege, seven had been killed and sixteen had died of sickness. In all, about four hundred Europeans were buried in that mournful cemetery in the compound; among them were Mr Polehampton, Mrs Clark of Gonda, Mrs Boileau's baby daughter, Robert Bartrum and Sir Henry Lawrence.

For the Englishwomen involved, the Relief of Lucknow marked the end of their active experience of the Mutiny. The military leaders simply wanted to get them out of the way fast so that their forces could get down to the business of ousting the rebels from Oudh. Campbell decided that four thousand men should remain at the Alambagh until more reinforcements arrived, while he, with a smaller force, should escort the non-combatants to safety. The ladies, travelling by hackery, bullock-cart or dhoolie, were hurried first to Cawnpore, where fighting was still going on in the surrounding districts. 'Nothing could look more wretched and miserable than this dreadful place as we came in by the light of the moon,' wrote Adelaide Case. 'The burnt bungalows, broken gates, the remains of gun-carriages, trees lying on the ground with their leaves and branches stripped off, and more than all, the thoughts which arose in our minds of the fearful scenes so lately enacted here, depressed and saddened us altogether.'

They were detained there for several days, longing to get away, and then were sent on to Allahabad, which they reached on 7th December. 'Here we met with such a welcome that it was almost overpowering,' wrote Katherine. 'Went with two other ladies to a house in Cantonments. It seemed strange to be in a comfortable house again, and have a room to myself; I could scarcely under-stand it. I could not realize the feeling of rest and security after all I had passed through . . . The weather is so lovely that we sit out of doors nearly all day in the garden. The scene around is very pretty, but it brings so vividly before me our dear little bungalow at Gonda that it makes my heart very sad – thinking of the days that are no more. We wander through the deserted houses around, most of which have been burnt to the ground; there are very few in Cantonments still standing. The church still remains, though most of the tablets have been torn off the walls. The scene of desolation which the place presents is very sad; so many happy homes having been utterly destroyed in the past year.'

For Katherine and the other widows left wandering aimless like refugees among such scenes of desolation, it must have seemed certain that the British way of life in India was at an end, or that, at least, it could never be at all the same again. But India is a large country, and there were hundreds of stations in the Presidencies of Bombay and Madras where every happy home was still intact, and the word 'Mutiny' had remained no more than a dark shudder beyond the horizon. And the British were a dogged and resilient people who were not about to abandon their rule and all the material benefits and challenges accruing to it just because a few battles had been lost, a few thousand British soldiers killed and a relatively small number of Englishwomen and children slaughtered. Whatever the cost of 1857 to the British, it was not too high a price to pay for the continuation and subsequent expansion of their imperial role in India.

PART THREE

Chapter Nine

On 8th November 1858 a manifesto was read aloud throughout British India which proclaimed that Queen Victoria had formally assumed the sceptre of power that had hitherto been wielded by her trustees, the East India Company. As Captain Trotter, a contemporary historian, described it, the occasion aroused general jubilation: 'In all the chief cities, the booming of guns, the clang of military music, cheers of paraded soldiery and the noise of admiring crowds acclaimed the new charter of Indian rights and aspirations. At night, both on land and water, there burst forth everywhere a blaze of fireworks, blue lights and the gleam of countless coloured lamps. Mosque, pagoda and Parsee temple vied with church in making night glorious in cities where gas was still unknown. Rejoicing crowds buzzed along the bazaars or blockaded with carriages the broader thoroughfares of the English town. There was feasting in the houses, not only of our own country folk, but of many a native gentleman in all parts of the country. Translated into twenty native tongues and reproduced in thousands of printed copies, the glad tidings proclaimed on that auspicious day speedily found an echo in the farthest corners of the Queen's new realm.'

The manifesto, being typical of its genre, contained many promises of a more glorious and prosperous future. 'Strong-handed peace', honest endeavour and just government would now prevail in the land; the 'rights, usages and customs' of the country would be legally safeguarded by its English rulers, as would the 'dignity and honour' of the Indian princes; 'natives of whatever race or creed' were to be freely admitted to public office; in short, all 'ranks and classes of Her Majesty's Indian subjects were assured of their ruler's protection and goodwill' – save only 'for the convicted murderers of English folk'.

There were some who realized that, for all its fine phrases, the document did not really embody any radical reforms from the paternal authoritarianism that had been the hall-mark of Company rule in its later period; but there were others who felt that the new approach was far too compromising and lenient – which was why the Queen's representative, India's first Viceroy, was dubbed 'Clemency' Canning. For the paramount British reaction to the Mutiny was a lust for immediate and sanguinary retribution, and the forces engaged in its mopping-up operations 'tranquillized the country by the very simple expedient of hanging everybody who showed signs of insubordination', according to George Trevelyan.

While this was going on, most of the survivors fled to the safety of the main cities, and, as one observer noted, 'Calcutta was full of refugees from the Upper Provinces, English officers and their wives who had escaped with their lives, but with the loss of every scrap of property . . . One body of these excited deep sympathy. It consisted entirely of ladies and children who had escaped from the state of Oudh. The husbands of many of them had been killed, those of others were detained on service. These poor creatures, after spending several months in the fort of Allahabad, had been sent to Calcutta by steamer. They had been in many cases obliged to flee for their lives only half-dressed and reached Calcutta in a state of complete destitution.' Lady Canning secured a large house for them all and provided caps and cuffs for the new widows. 'A good-hearted matron called Mrs Howe went round to all Europeans and collected not only money but old clothes and under-linen of all kinds. She might be seen in all corners of the town day after day with an old barouche piled high with clothes which she then distributed to the poor refugees. Then she would carry them off to the shops and make them happy buying gowns and bonnets for them.'

The urge for retribution was fed by such scenes as these and by numerous blood-chilling stories which circulated about the atrocities that some of the mutineers had committed. It was rumoured that white women had been raped, disembowelled, had their breasts or tongues cut off, that their children had been impaled on bamboo rods, buried alive or torn limb from limb on cart wheels. Fortunately the actual occurrence of these horrors was seldom proved, but they served to inflame public opinion in England and Anglo-India – particularly because the principal victims were said to have been women. The press in both countries waxed hysterical in demands for more severe punitive measures to be taken, and the rituals of revenge-killing were enacted even in the nurseries and schoolrooms of the homeland. 'I burnt and hanged and tortured the Nana Sahib in effigy many times,' remembered Flora Annie Steel in her autobiography written some sixty years later, by which time she had experienced at first hand many of the dramas and delights of the Indian scene. But when Flora and her brothers were playing mutiny games in their large country house in Scotland, she was a strong-willed irrepressible adolescent, and there was an interim of several years between her and India.

During those years – the early 1860s – the British regained and reinforced their control over the country by initiating some constitutional reforms and setting up more effective legal and administrative machinery. Nevertheless the mutiny left in its wake vibrations of uncertainty, fear and distrust that shuddered in the minds of Anglo-Indians for a generation and, as the *Times* journalist, W. H. Russell, wrote, 'produced too much hatred and ill-feeling between the two races to render any mere change of the name of the rulers a remedy for the evils which affect India'. These reactions were reinforced by the fact that no single cause for the outbreak was ever satisfactorily pinpointed: the British felt that if such a terrible catastrophe could occur once without anyone being quite sure why, something similarly awful could happen again, and with as little warning. So there was an edginess, an unease, a further widening of the divisions between rulers and ruled that had been growing for the past twenty years, which was accentuated by the prevalent British assumption of their destiny as a race born to govern and imperially command.

The attitudes of the memsahibs have customarily been quoted

as contributing largely to this undesirable development – though a more likely explanation is simply the rapid and considerable increase in their numbers. The presence of more wives meant that the domestic life of Anglo-Indian communities became more self-sufficient and elaborate, which further heightened their separation from India itself. As most mems. had scant opportunity for any personal contact with Indians, other than servants or tradesmen, they cannot be blamed too harshly for their opinions which were, indeed, often patronizing and ill-informed. For the average memsahib, whose own full personal and intellectual development had invariably been stunted by the restrictive conventions that Victorian England imposed on its womanhood, India was one enormous and continuing cultural shock, and many of them retreated from its impact into the relatively safe and very dull routines of small-station Anglo-India.

The majority of the stations were in the Bengal Presidency and the north-west, miles from any main-line rail or road communication. They were usually stuck in the heat-racked 'Sandy Tracts' as they were jokily called, and those who lived in them long enough were reputed to be prone to the disease called Sand in the Head. Its symptoms were complete mental befuddlement and chronic physical inertia; extreme cases were given to alcoholism or suicide; the only known cure was immediate removal to Malvern or Bath where the 'sand' could be washed away by the cooling Spa waters.

Certainly daily life in the moffusil (rural areas) must have been dreary and trying. Social contact revolved round the 'Assembly Room' where all main functions were held, from the weekend 'carpet hop' to the occasional Station Ball. In preparation for the latter, the floor was covered with white cloth stretched tight over the boards and rubbed with French chalk. Lizards were swept off the punkahs and spiders from the chandelier, and the colours of the resident regiment were hung on the walls. According to G. Atkinson, whose book *Curry and Rice* is full of satirical and amusing sketches of small-station life at the time, all the 'spins' from miles around would be corralled for the occasion – in particular demand were the rollicking ones, 'all giggles and gums', who bounced through every polka with the young ensigns. For there was still a shortage of marriageable white females in the moffusil, which meant that, according to one writer, 'to the elderly man and the clumsy terpsichorean male, the ball in India is a social ordeal of the most dismal character'.

Undoubtedly the men got their own back among themselves next morning, when they gathered in the one coffee-shop to smoke cheroots and comment on the 'feminine toilettes' of the previous night. Scene for the station's most exciting seasonal events was the race-course, consisting, wrote Atkinson, 'of at least three blades of auburn grass on every square foot of ground, and having the further advantage of being perforated with rat-holes'. It was also graced with a grandstand that 'exhibited the stern simplicity and severity of the primitive mound with the advantage of a gorgeously elaborate watch-tower'. The stand was for the hoi-poloi; the real ladies of the station sat in their buggies and carriages beside the rails to watch 'the rich blood of Old England's sons being proudly carried by the noble blood of Arabia's and India's steeds'.

Every station of middle size had its own hospital, court-room and church, 'a timber receptacle in the early-Indian ecclesiastical style usually known as Disappointed Gothic', a 'well-stocked burial ground' nearby, and, possibly a piece of open ground 'with five cabbages, three peach trees and a patch of onions known as the Botanical Gardens'. Along the main street, usually called The Mall, there were a few shops, customarily owned by Eurasians or Jews, according to Edward Braddon (another writer with first-hand experience of the moffusil scene), and selling 'wines, spirits, beer, antiquated oilmen's stores, salad oil bottled for many years like crusty old port, hermetically sealed fish that have been out of their native element for a lustrum or more, and a general assortment of articles of saddlery, hardware, ironmongery etc that may be some day rescued from the dust of ages by an adventurous purchaser'.

The 'Malls' were unpaved and had to be watered every afternoon so that the dust would not ruin the ladies' bonnets when they took their evening drives. It was not considered advisable to drive any wheeled vehicle in front of the Burra Bibbi of the station and so risk the despoliation of her bonnet, for the social scene was as status-ridden as the Hindu caste system. It was divided into three echelons: topmost, the members of the covenanted Indian Civil Service, headed by a Commissioner; next the 'military lines', whose commanding officer might be a colonel or brigadier; then 'the rest' – uncovenanted civilian officials, businessmen, missionaries, railway engineers, police superintendants, planters of tea, jute, indigo, with a number of clerks and shopkeepers clinging to the bottom rung. Some of the latter were Eurasian, called 'chee-chees' because of their rather indistinct accents; they were said to wear flashy clothes, possess unclean habits and were despised by both whites and educated Indians.

Ranking members of the civil and military communities would meet in smaller social gatherings – supper-parties, picnics, croquet and lawn tennis in the judge's compound – but the differences were not forgotten. Civilian wives, in the opinion of Julia Maitland who mixed with many of them in Madras, were 'generally very quiet, rather languid, speaking in almost a whisper, simply dressed, most always lady-like and *comme il faut*. Not pretty, but pleasant and nice-looking and rather dull, and give one very hard work in pumping for conversation.' Military wives, on the other hand, were considered rather fast, free and easy and noisy; married young, they were thus too early deprived of a mother's watchful care. Helen Mackenzie, who had much experience of them, deplored their habit of 'adopting the strange vocabulary of their husbands and their husbands' friends. It is common to hear ladies speaking not only of their husbands by their surnames (a thing unpardonable except of a peer) but of other guests in the same manner; talking of "our kit", "jolly", "pluck", "a cool thing" and other shocking phrases.' The ladies belonging to 'the rest' might, with luck, be invited to the Queen's Birthday Garden Party or the occasional all-station 'spread', at which, according to Atkinson, 'the incense of savory meats (which lie in hetacombs on the table) hang about like a London fog no punkah can disperse' and the ices 'relapse into tepid water' long before they are consumed.

The fancies and foibles commonly encountered among the moffusil mems. are amusingly caricatured by Atkinson. There was the judge's wife, whose main topic of conversation was the slowness of judiciary promotion so that she was a 'regular perambulating civil service compendium'; the magistrate's wife who disliked children, preferring 'a lapful of spaniels and a train of aides-de-camp; the colonel's wife, who on the contrary, had a 'quiverful' and a 'regiment' of tailors sitting on the verandahs all day making clothes and 'bottle-covers, pincushions, doillies, rugs and polka jackets' to be sold at the next Fancy Fair for the benefit of the local missionaries; and the Scotch doctor's wife who was so mean that she had her carriage pulled by a camel instead of a horse, and surreptitiously bought her underwear secondhand 'from the half-caste in the bazaar who sells to the soldiers' wives'.

With such pettifoggery were the marks of social caste observed, for there was little scope for proving one's superiority by the display of fine possessions or the provision of extra lavish hospitality. All the Anglo-Indian families lived in the simple cantonment bungalow – a rectangular block of rooms, each leading into the next, with concrete floors and whitewashed walls, usually with wire-netted slits cut high in them to let in some light and keep out mosquitoes. Outside, the bungalows were equally unlovely, 'all pillars, plaster and peagreen paint', says Atkinson, and surrounded by a shrivelled patch of ground where a few English flowers struggled pathetically to survive.

Because, as Honoria Lawrence had complained, people were always being moved from the pillars of one station to those of another, it was foolish to accumulate many household goods and it was customary to sell off some on departure and buy more on arrival at a new post. In consequence, furniture had a generally battered second-to-fifth-hand look about it, not improved by being plonked on ant-ravaged coconut matting or patchwork carpets made in the local gaol. Movable items – crockery, mirrors, cooking utensils – had been much moved, and were cracked, bent, chipped. In the living-rooms there was usually some chintz about, to fringe the punkah, cover the chairs, curtain the openings between rooms. But the bedrooms were quite spartan: wooden-frame bed laced with webbing; one thin cotton mattress; one sheet, and, often, a punkah draped with damp towels above the

147

bed that nearly swept the faces of the sleepers. A mere 'purdah' curtain divided them from the punkah-coolies and other staff on the verandah beyond – considering this general lack of privacy, allied to Victorian prudery, it seems rather surprising that Anglo-Indians managed to beget so many children. The only luxury of the sleeping quarters was a bathroom to every bedroom; it contained a zinc tub, earthenware jars of water and, often, fat pet lizards to eat the mosquitoes. Adjoining it was the 'retiring room', again a personal necessity, considering that there were no drains.

The pleasantest part of the bungalow was the verandah on to which all the main rooms opened. Bamboo screens between the pillars filtered the sun's glare there; at sunset, dogs lolled on the jackal-skin rugs, the sahib stretched his weary legs along the extended arms of the low chairs, the horse came begging for the evening lump of sugar. It was the best time of day; the sahib's wife, leaning on the verandah-rails, looked out over the pitiless sandy tracts on all the horizons and dreamed, perhaps, of the green Sussex Downs . . . and felt, perhaps, a little dreary.

According to one memsahib, Florence Marryat, who spent three years in the southern station of Bangalore, 'every sun set as it rose, and left a feeling behind it of an utterly wasted day, the description of one of which will serve for all'. Up at five o'clock, a ride on horseback till seven, 'little breakfast' on the verandah, a cold bath and dress ready to receive visitors. They came, inevitably, between ten and two o'clock, to chat and mutually commiserate. Then it was tiffin-time, followed by the siesta hour, 'drowsy, heavy, the sun at his meridian; every living creature out of doors has crept under shelter and a great silence pervades the whole cantonment'. She lay on her bed with a book till it was time to bath again, dress again, ride out again along the race-course and 'then to the band where, everybody being present, I could gossip to my heart's content until night-fall. Then there was the gallop home in the dark and, if there was any party to attend, dressing to be at once gone through; if not, a few songs sung, a good many yawns yawned and then bed until five the next morning when the whole business recommenced.'

That, for the great majority of wives, was the pattern of the days, varied only by the longed-for packet of letters from Home; the visits of itinerant traders selling Persian carpets, knick-knacks from Calcutta or offering to re-surface the kitchen utensils with copper; the killing of a sheep in the Mutton Club. Such a club, wrote Edward Braddon, 'is an institution in nearly every small station; one member, like Norval's father, feeds the flock and four or five members share the slaughtered animals; hind quarters, fore-quarters and saddles being distributed with fair alternation – save when a station dinner involves a departure from the ordinary sequence of joints.'

Thus the sequences of the moffusil: recurring baths and siestas, recurring taste of mutton and rice, recurring notes of the same polka, thunder of hooves on the race-course grit; the flat stare of the white bedroom walls, the same voices talking about Money, Promotion, Home; the same servants carrying water, sweeping refuse, dozing, like bundles of rags, in the verandah's shade; the sun, pitilessly high in the sky every day . . . A monotonous life, but a quiet one, easy to acquiesce in and sometimes enjoy. Most of the women expected no more than that.

But there were a few, endowed with above-average determination and energy, who sought to wrest more from their Indian experiences. One of them was Flora Annie Steel who, nine years after playing Mutiny games in the schoolroom, arrived in the land of the wicked Nana Sahib as the twenty-year-old wife of a member of the covenanted I.C.S. A conventional enough beginning, but the independence of her mind comes through at once in the way she describes that momentous joining: 'Why I married I cannot say. I never have been able to say. I do not think either of us was in love. I know I was not; I never have been.' This fact, she adds, though sad, never made life any the less full or entrancing for her; lacking the total commitment to any beloved one, she had instead an 'intense curiosity', an over-riding urge to understand her situation and do something practical with it.

Flora had several relatives in India and her husband, who was older than she, had already spent some years in the Service there. On their arrival, he was first posted to Ludhiana, where the Mackenzies had once raised a regiment, and where, in no time at all, Flora decided, as Helen Mackenzie had, that inefficiency and bungling was rife in all branches of the Indian administration. When her over-burdened husband fell ill, she wrote his reports for him. 'It was my first experience of government office,' she wrote, 'and it left me a confirmed Individualist for the rest of my life . . . The best form of Government is a beneficent Autocracy. Democracy went by the board as a thing of Mediocrity, the Apotheosis of Bureaucracy.' She may then have been, in her own words, 'a baby bride', 'round-faced, high-coloured, with my hair still in curls,' but she was a natural-born autocrat of a not entirely benevolent type, and she was never afraid to speak her mind.

Ludhiana was by then a middle-sized station and, as Flora says, had she remained there or at other comparable posts, she would have probably 'frittered away the time, joined an association or two . . . been full of good work and talk'. But after a year the Steels were sent to Kasur, a sub-division of the Lahore district that was in the Styx even by moffusil standards. For, 'at Kasur there was literally no one but the natives'. The town, formerly a Pathan settlement, was a collection of old brick houses, 'many-storied, purpled by age, set cheek by jowl and windowless; intersected by thread-like, tortuous, evil-smelling alleys'. The Steels, spared these, were housed in an old Mohammedan tomb with a large central dome to which six rooms had been attached. Mr Steel dispensed British justice from the cool, domed centre, and often Flora used to stop in its doorway, 'to listen to the monotonous echoing drawl of the sarishtadar (head clerk) read over some deposition. It was all so dim, so mysterious, so dignified; echoes might have reached high heaven.'

For Mr Steel then, the days were busy, if monotonous; for his young wife the problem of occupation was a difficult one. After the complicated birth of a daughter there was, she wrote, 'little hope of another child, and I had to map out my life as best I could'. By the age of twenty-four, she was 'mentally in that state of uncertainty about all things in which work seems the only anodyne – the one drug which enables you to present a bold front to your world'. And, she admits, 'but for the fact that, for a circle of some sixty miles in diameter I found myself absolutely alone, save for a busy husband, I should never have set myself to do the things I did'.

The first thing she did was to try and acquire some knowledge of the local vernaculars, and by so doing opened several opportunities for herself of which only a few foreigners bothered to avail themselves. One of the main reasons why so many Englishwomen remained bored strangers in a strange land for years on end was their inability to communicate interestingly with Indians. It was a grave omission; only partly excusable on the grounds that some husbands positively discouraged their families from learning any native tongue because of its 'impropriety'.

Once Flora had picked up a smattering of the language, her enjoyment of the Inspection Tours that she and her husband made was greatly enhanced. To her receptive eye, the low-lying plains round the River Sutlej were strange and beautiful. 'I see the procession now as we started from our over-night camp in the early morning,' she wrote. 'The sky a fair sapphire and set in a frame of gold, for the mustard is in bloom. Far away, a glint of silver; nearer at hand, still pools where egrets stand watchful.'

Greeted by the elders of a village, she used to listen with fascination to the disputes that arose over the apportioning and measuring of fields and boundaries. As the quiet voices droned on, she would sometimes wander off and sit, 'watching God's beautiful world as it stretches out before me to a horizon of grey-green tamarisk, yellow sand strips and wisps of green catch-crops here and there'. A flock of flamingoes streaked rosepink in the distance, and she heard the 'sibilant hiss of the grey lag goose sentinel as he gives warning of strangers'. Gathered round the village wells in the evenings, 'what tales can you not hear . . . details of the peasants' hopes and fears and doubts' – how this one had his best acre swamped in last year's floods, that one had fifty-three head of cattle stolen one night and nothing but the corpses of two calves left for him to pick up in the morning.

Back in Kasur, Flora's main delight was her garden that surrounded the old tomb and the 'road garden' her husband had laid out along the town's main thoroughfare. When the Steels arrived, Kasur was very dry and barren, its average annual rainfall being but 13 inches, and what water there was 'brought to the surface by means of a deep well, a skin bag and oxen, apparently only succeeded in bringing borate of soda with it'. Mr Steel, 'a lineal descendant of Adam', remedied this by having a channel cut from the big canal near Lahore to bring fresh water to the town. After that, gardening became fashionable and patches of grass, roses, jasmine and dracaenas flourished along the roadsides.

On Sunday afternoons, Kasur's Municipal Committee assembled in the Steels' court-house garden for informal discussions on local affairs. There were about a dozen members and its vice-president was 'a courteous, small, spare old man with a hawk face and close white beard' who had, in his youth, been fencing master to Ranjit Singh. In due course the full committee would 'with immensely long Persian salutations take its departure behind some flowering shrubs. Thence it would emerge as the Sanitation sub-committee, in number reduced to three, and would discourse learnedly about saucer drains and sweepers' brooms. This, in turn, would with infinite politeness and ceremonial, disappear behind the flowering shrubs to give place to the Education sub-committee which – to please me of course – would discuss in the most flowery of Persian the necessity of educating women. They in their turn would be replaced by the Garden sub-committee (to please my husband) and so on and on. The remainder, discreetly hidden by the shrubs, would be eating iced melon and cold plum pudding.'

The ice was sent by special post from Lahore and the pudding had been in continuing popular demand ever since Flora gave them a piece to try at Christmas. Two of the pudding's important ingredients – beef suet and brandy – were not locally obtainable, but undoubtedly Flora's version was delicious, for she was a creative and versatile cook. Indeed she was a wizard in all the domestic arts, and while she was living in Kasur, she began the compilation of her personal experience and advice on the subject that later appeared as *The Complete Indian Housekeeper and Cook*, dedicated to those 'English Girls to whom Fate may assign the task of being Housemothers in our Eastern Empire'.

The book, as Flora explains in its preface, was intended as a practical guide for all the young memsahibs who, upon arriving in India, found themselves bereft of all 'the familiar landmarks' of efficient housewifery. 'The kitchen is a black hole, the pantry a sink. The only servant who will condescend to tidy up is a skulking savage with a reed broom; whilst pervading all things broods the stifling, enervating atmosphere of custom, against which energy beats itself unavailingly as against a feather-bed.' The typical Indian servant, when not actually a savage, was certainly always 'a child in everything save age and should be treated as a child; that is to say, kindly but with the greatest firmness'. Flora recommends that a 'system of rewards and punishments' be adopted to educate the staff in 'some sense of duty' and that the truly incorrigible should be dosed with castor oil 'on the ground that there must be some physical cause for inability to learn or remember'.

Faced with such appalling domestic arrangements, so much human frailty, the memsahib's only remedy is to equip herself with sufficient knowledge to assert her authority and bring Western-style order out of Eastern-style chaos. Accordingly, Flora's book tells all: the Tamil word for horse-barley and the Urdu for colander; the price of a cane chair in Bombay or a dozen eggs in the moffusil; the implements to be supplied to house-bearers (to include twelve soft dusters, scissors, corkscrew, ice-breaker and a tin of Putz Pomade); the cost of hiring a bullock-drawn transit van in Ootacumund or a water-carrier in Bengal; how to build a camp-oven from a round sheet-iron drum and three bricks; the best way of making snipe pudding, 'cannibal broth' for invalids, mange ointment for dogs; the customary duties of an ayah (to include bringing morning tea, brushing the memsahib's hair, laying out her walking boots and parasol); how much corn meal to give the hens per day and how many pairs of calico combinations to take to the Punjab; tips on the nursing of those suffering from fever, dysentery, sunstroke or dyspepsia; how to clarify butter, pack a piano, remove ticks from guinea-fowl; the correct quantities of fish oil, mutton suet and resin for boot-dubbin, and of linseed oil, turpentine and raw opium for dosing a cow with colic; the correct method of using Berkefeld's Patent Travellers and Army Pump Filter and of loading Camel Number

Nine when going on a three-month visit to the hills; the relative merits of cows', goats' or asses' milk for nursing babies; how to preserve leather, get rid of white ants, treat prickly heat, clean lampwicks and palm-leaf matting, make a cholera belt, kill snakes, cure the squeak of a punkah, keep sparrows out of a sick-room, judge the competence of a syce, rear quails in a pit.

Then, and in particular, were instructive chapters on gardening and cookery, Flora's two special enthusiasms. A typical mali (gardener) had no true sympathy with plants, she declared firmly, and should be regarded merely as an instrument for carrying out orders. Nor did he have any notion of the art of transplanting, preferring to 'sit down contentedly in the sun with a basket of young lettuce plants and proceed to slide along in a sitting posture, leaving a curious plantigrade trail behind him, bordered on either side by dejected little lettuces thrust into the ground by one swift action of his thumb'. This sort of behaviour – together with other lamentable habits such as sowing the whole garden with radishes at one time or spending too many hours on the bullock's back watering instead of getting down to the nitty-gritty of weeding – had to be 'exterminated if good crops are to result'.

The memsahib of the garden also had her duties – to arrange for ample stocks of good half-rotted manure from the cowshed and stables, to order first-class seeds from Home, to supply proper wooden labels for the crop-rows, not little 'scraps of paper which the first inquisitive parrot or squirrel makes off with'. Needless to say, the several gardens over which Flora presided flourished exceedingly; she grew all the usual English vegetables and her flower-beds were a country-cottage composition of hollyhocks and candytuft, sweet peas and stocks, geraniums and snap-dragons.

Kitchens and cooks also blossomed under her command. The former had to be 'airy and wholesome' with floors of 'broad flat bricks such as are used for mosques and public buildings, set close in really good mortar'. The latter were tractable, providing they could be purged of all those 'dirty habits which are ingrained in the native cook' – such as stirring eggs in the rice pudding with his finger, straining soup through his turban – and of certain 'delusions'

– such as that a sheep's head must always be skinned when it is to be potted. A good cook, Flora explained, must always work methodically to a fixed programme. His first job of the day should be to order the sweeper to remove yesterday's ashes from the stove and the bhisti to refill the water pots; then he should attend to the accounts (with due regard to the 'words of the Koran about not disobeying your faith for the sake of a few pice'), and ordering the day's supplies in consultation with the mistress of the house. At that stage, he might, if he must, have a smoke providing he kept his hookah out of the kitchen; then it was time to whip up a caramel custard from the left-over skim milk, rub down the pickled meats, make sure that the stock-pot was topped up with bones and vegetable scraps before the real cooking of the day was embarked upon.

Considering that all the cooking was carried out on an open-fire charcoal range with an oven beside, in a cook-house that was usually situated a good fifty yards from the main living quarters, and that many Indian servants were quite unaccustomed to western-style eating habits, the culinary expectations and demands of the Anglo-Indian household were high. Flora inveighed against the 'detestable fashion' of serving five- or six-course tiffins at which the eaters were 'stuffed into a semi-torpid state' that was not conducive to scintillating conversation, these followed a few hours later by pretentious, badly cooked dinners 'in the style of a third-class French restaurant' and ending with a dessert that became 'a *troisième service*' with too many sweet wines and 'the khitmagars prancing round with distracting chocolates, pralines or pickled ginger' as the ladies staggered off to the drawing-room.

This tendency towards increasingly lavish display was, in her view, both tasteless and unhealthy. Better to have bright glass, shining silver, crisp white napkins 'with some backbone' than elaborate table decorations and pats of butter that have obviously and touchingly been 'the medium for a display of the khitmagar's power in plastic art'; better to have a clear and wholesome broth than those glutinous and over-rich compounds beloved by the domestics; better to have a cook who knows how to prepare delicious dishes from fresh vegetables than one who is always 'bleating for truffles and cream and butter and champagne and goodness knows what'.

All this domestic sagacity did not descend upon Flora overnight, for her book was the distillation of twenty-two years experience of India, and, as she later wrote, she took 'a immense o' trouble' over it. Her pains were rewarded – the book ran into ten editions and, she wrote proudly, she had 'letters without end thanking me for it, from housekeepers, gardeners, cow-keepers and chicken-rearers'. She had Kasur to thank for most of her livestock-rearing experience, and it was there that she became a dab hand at the making of float whey, hatted kit and rennet curd from the daily dairy products.

After her supervision of the domestic scene, Flora turned her attention to community affairs. The Municipal Council, emboldened by many helpings of melon and plum pudding at the chief Sahib's residence, 'was beginning to feel itself of some consequence' and wanted a more dignified building for the exercise of its several offices. So Mrs Steel designed a new Town Hall for them – an elaborate edifice with a large arched apse on one side. The Council approved of the plan and sent it to the Department of Public Works, who returned it with a veto on the apse and 'in its stead a very creditable drawing of a Swiss chalet'. But the Council still preferred Flora's design and had it built anyway, at less cost than the 'Swiss chalet' and with a circular verandah in tiers so that the top officials could sit at a higher level than their underlings, which, as Flora pointed out, was sensibly 'in deference to the ingrained sense of caste'.

So what with all that, and airing her views in a Lahore newspaper about the oppression of small land-holders by usurers, and making a tour of Kashmir and nursing her husband through several bouts of fever (the chief work of the nurse, whether skilled or unskilled 'is to make the moral, mental and physical atmosphere of the sick room as peaceful and hopeful as possible', she pronounced), the time of her departure from Kasur came almost too soon. To express their appreciation of her efforts, the townspeople gathered in the new Town Hall, its apse decorated with Chinese lanterns, and presented her with a large brooch, every jewel in it taken from those worn by the local wives. She was very moved, tried to speak, cried. 'And so mercifully did everyone else. We wept profusely. That then is my farewell to Kasur. I doubt if anyone ever had a better keepsake given them. I used to call it my Star of India.' The year was 1876, Flora Annie was twenty-nine years old, no longer quite the 'baby bride', rather an opinionated and assured young woman, but still as eager and determined as a child to glean all she could from the experience of India.

Chapter Ten

There was another matter to which Flora Annie Steel turned her indefatigable attention while she was living in Kasur, and which occupied more of her interest in later years – the education of the Indian female. The whole question of education was a controversial one in Anglo-Indian circles, and had been since the 1820s, when high-minded Englishmen with humanitarian ideals began to consider the 'general elevation of the native mind'. Most of the early educational institutions for Indians were established by Christian missionaries, but from the first there was disagreement as to which language should be the principal medium of instruction and which classes of Indian society should benefit most from the resources available. Although, during the 1850s and 60s, the government tried to broaden the base of educational opportunity, the great majority of those who received any form of higher education were from the middle and upper classes, and nearly all of them were male. For, as Flora found out in Kasur, 'the inborn aversion to female education' was still very strong.

However, with her forceful encouragement, Kasur's Municipal Council agreed to start a school and 'two or three dozen little girls from the bazaar ranging from four to eight years were duly installed in the alphabet class' held in a courtyard under the instruction of a 'toothless male, neutrally religious' who would not offend either Moslem or Hindu. Following this reasonably successful experiment, Flora's enthusiasm for the cause increased, and when, after leaving Kasur, the Steels were posted to several larger stations in the north-west, her husband got busy with the planting of road-side gardens and she with the opening of girls' schools, which, 'given a municipal council and an ex-officio president with a will towards female education . . . were the quickest crop to sprout'.

In due course and rather reluctantly, her efforts gained a certain degree of government recognition and when her husband was again moved to 'a civilized district near Lahore', she was offered the post of 'Inspectress of Female Schools'. She felt bound to accept because, she claimed, 'I was indeed the only woman in the Punjab outside the ranks of mission ladies who could read and write the vernaculars'. Her inspection area covered some five hundred miles between Peshawar and Delhi and she spent much of her time on horseback and in railway carriages. After a long overnight journey, she found it a great pleasure 'on a crisp, clear winter's morning, or even a balmy summer's dawn, to walk through the wheat fields near the town and be met down some alley with the chanting of Sanskrit hymns or the murmured intoning of the Koran; for, though it was strictly against the rules, I always allowed an extra hour in my particular schools for instruction in the pupils' religion'.

A committed, but not a proselytizing, Christian herself, she created her first 'outcry' on the educational scene by refusing to grant government aid to any school which actually paid its pupils to attend – though this was fairly common missionary practice in the East at that time. She created another furore by trying to abolish the system of awarding annual prizes to every pupil whatever their individual attainments, for she believed, with children as with servants, that only virtue and distinction should be rewarded. Eventually she created real trouble for herself when she pressed for a formal enquiry into rumours of malpractice in the organization of Lahore University. As a result, she wrote, 'a cabal' was formed against her and 'one false charge after another was trumped up'. Then her husband was posted to a remote out-station in order that she and her pertinacious zeal might also be removed. 'I suppose I was over cocksure,' she wrote. 'I have always been told that it has been my weakness and strength all my life.'

Not surprisingly, for many less able and industrious men and their unobtrusive wives must have been infuriated by Mrs Steel's bossy, insistent energy and her confident assertion of her own powers – especially as they were housed in a distinctly rotund and unimpressive female form. Not that she was ever worried by adverse comment. 'I think the cause of humanity's mock modesty is really the underlying, yet totally unfounded belief that everybody must like you,' she wrote. 'Now there is no proposition more untrue than this. It is quite impossible that everybody will like you, unless, indeed, you are a mere nonentity.'

No one could accuse Flora Annie of being that. In due course her suspicions of the maladministration at Lahore proved justified and she was summoned to Simla and 'solemnly white-washed by staying in Government House'. Its incumbent at the time was Lord Dufferin, who apparently found her most entertaining and, she wrote, 'nearly fell off his chair with laughing at the Infant Phenomenon, a favourite impersonation of mine, for which my round face and high colour suited me'. Returned to the plains, she resumed her Inspectress duties and became the first woman member of the Punjabi Education Board. Her last act, on leaving India when her husband retired, 'was to promise to write for the Board a primer on Hygiene for the Girls' Middle School examination to take the place of the perfectly useless Euclid'.

After leaving India, incidentally, Mrs Steel continued to make her presence felt. She wrote several popular novels set in the country – the best known, *On the Face of the Waters*, was heralded at the time as a 'classic as long as the Indian Mutiny is remembered'. Maud Diver, the author of *Englishwomen in India*, a book of admonition and exhortation to females bound for an imperial destiny in the East, paid tribute to Flora as one 'rare as she is admirable' – a shining example that 'might well prove profitable and stimulating' to lesser memsahibs. 'What though they be incapable of the achievement attained by Mrs Steel's unconquerable energy, they may at least contribute their mite toward increasing that love and respect for the British Raj which it is the duty of every English man and woman in India to uphold,' Mrs Diver concluded. Nevertheless, the name of Flora Annie Steel awakened mixed reactions from the Anglo-Indian community, partly because she had the incorrigible habit of suggesting that she, and only she, was actually coping competently with the various causes she espoused. It is unlikely, for instance, that she was truly the only non-missionary lady in the Punjab 'with a grasp of the vernaculars', and she was certainly not the only one concerned about the education of Indian girls.

The concept of mass education gained ground in mid-Victorian England and dreams of the eventual millennium of Universal Literacy began to spread to the Empire. Lord Mayo, who was Viceroy of India from 1869 to 1872, was a keen educationalist who expressed the aim of 'teaching the 3 R's to rural Bengal'. During his term of office more government funds were diverted into primary education, though still little was done to instruct girls, for fear of offending the conservative prejudices of Hindu and Moslem. A few Indian men themselves however began to profess anxiety about the backward state of their young womenfolk, and even visited England in the hope of gaining support for the changes they wanted to make in Indian society – such as the abolition of child marriages and of the keeping of women in conditions of ignorant seclusion.

One of these was a Mr Keshub Chunder Sen of the Indian Reform Association who, on 1st August 1870, at a meeting of the Victoria Discussion Society in London, made an impassioned plea for the services of 'well-trained, accomplished English ladies' who would be prepared to go to India and offer to 'their Indian sisters' an education 'that will not be subservient or subordinated to the views of any particular religious community, an education free and liberal and comprehensive in character, calculated to make Indian women good wives, mothers, sisters and daughters'. It was stirring stuff and several of those present responded eagerly, though few were actually fired into later action.

But there was a young lady, not at the meeting, who studied Mr Sen's speech afterwards in the quiet of her Stourbridge home, and let its contents seep meaningfully into her mind. Her name was Annette Ackroyd, a resolute personality, who, having received an excellent education herself by the standards of the time, pondered the situation of intelligent girls who had not been offered her chances. She was involved in the founding of the first

Working Women's College in London in 1854 and began teaching there in 1871, soon after Keshub Sen's visit to England. Her interest in Indian affairs had sprung from her family's strong humanitarianism – for the Unitarians were in the forefront of the movement towards progressive colonial reform. While working at the College her interest in the movement crystallized into a determination to go to India to teach those even more unfortunate millions of 'Hindu sisters' who were purportedly clamouring for instruction.

Annette was then twenty-nine years old, a 'little, soft, white-skinned, wee woman', in the words of one of several friends who tried to convince her that she was far too frail and sensitive for such an undertaking. For, at that time, very few of the English women who went to India were single, unless they were going to join their families, or were affiliated to educational or religious bodies. But Annette was adamant. Her beloved father, William, had recently died; her stepmother was not greatly attached to her; she had wasted part of her youth in the provincial social rounds of Stourbridge where there were no young men of equal intellect to sweep her off her feet. So it was time to sweep herself off and make her own mark on the other side of the world. She took lessons in Bengali and a course in the teaching of young females; she sailed in October 1872 and reached Calcutta in December, just after her thirtieth birthday.

Annette was aware that her self-appointed task would not be easy, but she had not fully anticipated the extent of the difficulties and hostilities she would encounter. She was convinced that the western-style education offered to Indians should be exclusively secular, which meant that she could not hope for the support – and indeed aroused the antagonism of – all the Christian-based educational institutions in Calcutta. Nearly all their teachers were, she decided, 'ignorant and conceited' people, much more concerned with the numbers of their supposed converts than the quality of their instruction.

The attitude of the missionaries was predictable, but she had not expected that the rest of her compatriots would be so insular and intolerant in their views. The more she mixed in Anglo-Indian society, the more she became 'convinced of the falseness of our position here . . . I sit among a group of ladies and hear one lisping to a gentleman her complaint that the natives come so early, sit downstairs in the ante-room with their feet on the sofa in the oriental fashion as if they were at home . . . I hear at Belvedere of ladies who say, "Ah no I never spoke to a native" when asked to help to entertain and talk to some of the numerous Indians present, and another who said, "Let us sit on the verandah to get out of the natives." Such sentiments gave her 'a sickening heart-ache and terror of life here. How these sweet and feminine souls, whose sympathy is so tender and sensibilities so acute, can be so destitute, not only of humanity, but of simple courtesy and consideration of the feelings of others, is a problem I cannot pretend to solve.'

However, Annette was not totally alone in her reactions of dismay and disgust at this state of affairs. The *Times of India*, in an editorial written a year before her arrival, pressed for the admission of more Indians to the ranks of the covenanted Civil Service and deplored the fact 'that it is the tone of English society to look down upon people of the country as at the best amiable dupes and men whose opinions of state questions or general topics are worthless'. It was more than time, the paper declared, for the British to re-appraise thoroughly their approach to India and translate into action some of the fine promises about more democratic opportunity and prosperity for the masses that had been made when the Crown took over official control of the government. A minority, though not at the time a very vocal one, shared these liberal views, and it was among them, naturally, that Annette found support and help for her educational scheme, that was intended, in its small way, to help break down the barriers between the 'natives' and the lisping white ladies on the verandahs.

Unfortunately, however, though all her initial sympathies were on the side of the Indian reformers, she soon discovered that they were very inconsistent and divided among themselves. Mr Keshub Sen proved to be untrustworthy and dangerous, a man who did not in the least practise what he preached as his own wife was illiterate and secluded, and she played with her jewels 'like a foolish petted child' when Annette visited her. When Annette attended one of Mr Sen's meetings in Calcutta she found herself 'the only lady' present and thus very much the object of the curiosity and 'impertinence' of some two thousand or so Bengali males in the audience. She was soon forced to admit that the men's attitude towards women was profoundly 'uncivilized' and that, by trying to educate Hindu girls for the wider world, she was up against very deeply rooted male prejudice.

So it was against this unsatisfactory and depressing background that Annette tried to organize her first girls' school in Calcutta. She had to start from scratch. She circulated subscription lists to raise funds, and many entries in her diary of early 1873 read simply, 'Looking for houses'. Landlords, she discovered, seldom meant what they said; neither did the committee of Bengali gentlemen formed to help in the school's launching, though they overwhelmed her with instruction and advice. One wanted her to teach singing and dancing to her pupils, though, as she knew, such pursuits were considered disreputable attainments for females by most Hindus; another protested against her plan of teaching the girls to use knives and forks, and she agreed to 'have a separate table for finger-users if necessary'; a third wanted her to make the girls some semi-western-style clothes, while another vowed to leave the committee and denounce her in the newspapers if they wore anything other than their traditional native dress.

She was denounced by the local Indian press anyway, and 'Oh, what a time of misery I have passed,' she wrote in June 1873 when the columnists' attacks upon her began. They said she had been starving in England and came to Calcutta to make money for herself; they said she wanted to convert her pupils into 'infidels'; they said she was a woman 'in an unmarried state, which is contrary to religion' and that 'the instructions of a person in such a condition are therefore not to be accepted'. 'What improvement of Hindu women can be effected by an Englishwoman?' they asked. 'What does she know of our social customs that our women should be really elevated by her instruction?' And, 'Are our women really so degraded that there is no other object to which compassion can be extended?' In short, the very last thing most Indian men wanted was for their daughters to be indoctrinated with the customs of the white foreigners: 'We have seen that the wives of all Europeans who live here are utterly shameless. Where women cast off their modesty and associate with men, that which principally constitutes female virtue is destroyed.'

Annette stuck bravely to her guns. 'I care no more for them than for the flies walking in the room below,' she wrote home to her sister, Fanny, who was quite shocked at the amount of adverse attention she had aroused. But, Annette declared, 'I've got used to seeing my name in print, though at first I did think it very dreadful.' And it must have been some comfort to her when, at the height of the controversy, she received a letter, with a decorated border, signed by 'A Hundred and Ten Bengallee Gentlemen' who wanted to express their sense of obligation to her 'for the zealous interest always felt by you in the welfare of our local institutions, as for the benevolent objects of your sojourn in our country generally'. But she remained distressed and hurt by the opposition and her hopes of gaining the sympathy and cooperation of India's menfolk were badly shaken, even though she persevered.

Early in the autumn she at last managed to rent a house in Baniapookur Lane, Calcutta – a 'dreadful lane, full of ditches and right-angled turnings'. She moved in at once to supervise the necessary white-washing and repairs, and begin 'doing all a shocked foreigner could do to make the men do their work a little more honestly'. She foraged for furniture round the Bow Bazaar, where, according to Sara Duncan, a more light-hearted memsahib, 'all things are of honourable antiquity . . . Three-legged memorials of old Calcutta, springless, oval-backed sofas that once upheld the ponderous dignity of the East India Company, tarnished mirrors which may have reflected the wanton charms of Madame le Grand . . . They stand huddled in little hot low-roofed shops, intimate with common teakwood things of yesterday, condescending to gaudy Japanese vases and fly-blown prints and cracked lamps and mismatched crockery.' Annette, raw in knowledge and poor in purse, picked what she could from the motley collection, had great difficulty in finding water filters, was dismayed at the delays in getting things delivered. Reliable servants were another scarcity, and she was obliged to employ a rather troublesome 'orthodox widow' as housekeeper 'who will have to have fresh flowers brought her each day as an offering to her "idol" and mustn't be touched while eating'. All in all, 'you can have no concept of the *worry* of India', she told Fanny.

Eventually on 18th November, the Hindu Mahila Bidyalaya (Hindu Ladies' School) was opened, with Annette at its head, one assistant mistress, a pundit and about ten pupils. It was a tough, lonely grind, week after week in Baniapookur Lane with the muddle and filth of India only just kept at bay, and with no one on the spot to whom she could confide all her worries and uncertainties. The school's curriculum was framed, as she had intended, on lines of strict theological neutrality, though it included something 'of high moral tone' to be read to the girls every day. Most basic subjects were taught, including Moham-medan history which Annette was 'very glad' she did not have to learn herself; there was reading in Bengali and English and 'great attention was given to the training of the pupils in practical house-work and to the formation of orderly and industrious habits'. Annette also tried to broaden her pupils' horizons by taking them to Fine Art Exhibitions, Magic Lantern Shows and the Botanical Gardens. 'Most of the girls had *never* walked so far before,' she exclaimed.

The financial situation of the school improved slightly as more pupils appeared, but poor Annette still found them impossible to know truly. One day none of them would eat, and they refused to tell her why; later she heard it was because a sweeper of the untouchable caste had been seen entering the kitchen. Glasses full of milk were placed under her table every morning, she never could discover the reason. 'It is like living among quicksands,' she wrote in her journal. She visited her Bengali neighbours and tried to interest the womenfolk in her ideas. But, she confessed, 'I am so tired of always taking the initiative and crave the refreshment of being talked to.' Most of the women were 'too inert or careless to carry on topics of conversation' and 'their minds are like india-rubber balls – you make a slight dent and then they return to a dull neutral-coloured, soul-depressing surface'. Eight months after the school opening she wrote sadly in her journal, 'As for the widespread desire for the education of women – it does not exist'.

Occasionally she escaped – to a public lecture at the Central Library, a Musical Evening or a week's holiday with her kind and sympathetic friends, the Phears and the Hobhouses. And doubtless she put up a brave front to them, as she did in her letters home. 'You must not think I am *really* unhappy or ill,' she reassured Fanny, who had recently married. She was wiser now, better able to cope and 'I shrink from the memory of how ignorant I was when I first came'. But with experience came disillusion: 'Oh dear, there is no concealing the fact that, with few exceptions, it is well to have as little to do with Bengalis as possible. – There, you see what eighteen months of intimate knowledge has brought me to,' she admitted in the summer of 1874. In that frame of mind she badly needed to get away from the school for a while, but she had no close friend to whom she could entrust its affairs, and she was trapped by the bitter realization that, if she did leave, the whole project might collapse. But early the following year her true friend arrived, and that meant the end of the school.

His name was Henry Beveridge, a member of the covenanted I.C.S., who first went out to India in the year of the Mutiny when he was twenty. He was a widower, his young wife, Jeannie, having died in India, and he had first made Miss Ackroyd's acquaintance through Jeannie's mother who had travelled to the country on the same ship as Annette. Henry Beveridge was a convinced agnostic, an intelligent and committed humanitarian, which resulted in his taking an active interest in Annette's school; his name appears on its first Subscription List and he was on the Managing Committee. So he had been waiting in the wings, as it were, from the beginning – writing encouraging letters, warning Miss Ackroyd, on one occasion, about the danger of 'being too much identified with the anglicized Bengalis'.

His station was six days' journey from Calcutta, so the two seldom met until he called to see her at the school in February 1875, on his way home on furlough. After visiting her five times he proposed to her – backing his offer with a letter that contained a reasoned discussion of John Stuart Mill's views on matrimony, and a candid appraisal of his family commitments and future prospects. He concluded that his proposal was 'an imperfect gift . . . If you accept it I shall be glad, but I would rather that you should not accept it in ignorance of its imperfections.'

She was in a dilemma; he wanted to marry her at once and carry her back to England; she temporized, thinking of the school, of how strong and single she had intended to remain. When they 'came to an understanding' she wrote to him, 'Do you know that I think it very fatiguing to be engaged to be married in addition to teaching English?' They were both mature people and each had compromises and adjustments to make. She wanted to keep her own name and be Mrs Ackroyd-Beveridge; he agreed heartily, saying, 'I don't at all approve of merging a wife's individuality in the husband's.' He refused to have a church wedding and insisted they be joined by a civil ceremony. Annette was sweetly vanquished: 'I never had my own way so little in my life,' she wrote. 'It is quite a novelty to feel that I don't belong to myself.'

On 5th April she left the school in Baniapookur Lane and soon after the venture closed. She and Henry were married at the Registration Office in Larkin's Lane under Act Three of 1872 declaring that they did not profess 'the Christian, Jewish, Hindu, Mohammedan, Parsi, Buddhist, Sikh or Jaina religion'. They were among the first couples to do so and the Act became popularly known afterwards as the 'Beveridge Act'. Not the Ackroyd-Beveridge Act, for Annette had lost her name and her economic independence, as was practically inevitable for a married woman in her time. But she never totally submerged her personality in Henry's, and the two of them – as partners, lovers, friends – had many years of Indian experience together.

Chapter Eleven

The last part of the Victorian Age was the period of the High Raj; its inauguration trumpeted and defined by Disraeli's Bill for investing the British sovereign with the formal title of Empress of India. The event prompted a fanfare of festival durbars in the main cities of the country, the grandest of them at Delhi, where thousands gathered on the sandstone Ridge that had once been the scene of so much battle agony. Among the visitors to the Ridge, incidentally, was Harriet Tytler, with her husband Robert, and it gave her a very peculiar feeling indeed to discover, amid the splendour of the vast vice-regal camp, that little bell-of-arms tower still standing and being used as a temporary living-room for some of the guests. It had been fitted with glass windows and the bullet holes in its walls had been effaced, 'so that I could hardly recognize in its new state of grandeur our former humble little home shelter'. Several others among the festive crowds must have been similarly haunted by the stark and queasy memories of twenty years before; but it was as well not to dwell on them anymore, when the only guns fired at Delhi on New Year's Day 1877 were in salutation.

On that day, Lord Lytton, the reigning Viceroy, 'took the central seat of dignity on a dais in front of a resplendent semi-circle of princes, grandees, courtiers, standard bearers and ladies seated or standing in due order of rank and precedence to hear the proclamation of the new title which the Queen of England had deigned to assume', wrote Captain Trotter. He then scathingly suggested, as did *The Times* of London, that the whole affair was little more than a gimmick intended to captivate the native population and frighten the Russians, and that 'the Viceroy's weakness for all kinds of decorative show and glitter made him a ready and useful instrument for carrying out Lord Beaconsfield's designs'.

Certainly Lord Lytton was a lover of pomp and circumstance. 'In the early days of his rule,' commented Trotter, 'he gratified his theatrical tastes by a noteworthy reform in the fashions of feminine dress. Former viceroys had been content to open their drawing-rooms to English ladies attired in the customary garments of their day. But Lord Lytton issued a decree that all ladies who wished to attend the State Receptions at Government House should wear long trains, after the manner of European courts. The innovation was generally condemned as costly, needless and vexatious; but it pleased Lord Lytton to invest his office with all the ceremonial splendour that beseemed the Vice-Regent of so great a sovereign as the Empress of Hindustan.'

So that was the prevailing tone – the dignity and grandeur of India's rulers were to be flaunted at whatever cost to individual comfort and economy. And the Anglo-Indian woman, proud symbol of British power over the land, was to be adorned ever more luxuriously and extravagantly in the imperial cause. Charles Buckland, in his *Social Life in India* of the period, describes those stately Government House levees when all the ladies who 'had the private entrée' were arranged, obediently en train, 'in a sort of sacred semi-circle on either side of the Vice-Regal throne'. Following the audience, they were ushered into the large drawing-rooms, where 'long buffets are laid out with everything that is needed to refresh them after their exertions'. An excellent arrangement, he comments, 'as it affords them a suitable opportunity to display their dresses and see their friends' dresses and receive the admiration to which they are entitled'.

And certainly it was exhausting to be within the sacred viceregal circle at the summit of so much imperial circumstance. Viceroys had less personal authority in the making of long-term political decisions than the governor-generals of pre-Mutiny days, but they were still called upon to decide, preside over and judge a great range of internal legal and financial affairs, however scant their first-hand experience of the country. A viceroy, noted a contemporary satirist, 'who is the axis of India, the centre round which the Empire rotates, is necessarily screened from all knowledge of India'. The screening was effected partly by the considerable dignity of office, which involved both viceroy and vicereine in a continual round of ceremonial functions. And, to judge by the account given in Lady Dufferin's *Our Vice-Regal Life in India*, the pace was so hectic as to make Emily Eden's experience of her somewhat similar position fifty years before sound like a sinecure.

The Dufferins accepted their lot with cheerful stamina and their period of office, though unremarked for any drastic reforms, was characterized by a certain confident and relaxed efficiency. They had experience of the job, for since their marriage in 1862 they had been posted to various imperial outposts, including Canada, where Lord Dufferin was Viceroy during the 1870s. He had an appropriately aristocratic mien – drooping moustache, elegant clothes and an aloof air that melted on better knowing. His wife, Harriot Georgina, eldest daughter of an Anglo-Irish landowner, was also attractive in a cool, contained way, with intelligent eyes and, as her husband once wrote, an air of 'gentle but persistent authority' that was quite effective.

The Dufferins arrived in Calcutta on 13th December 1884, accompanied by their three daughters, and Dufferin was immediately sworn in as the eighth Viceroy. The ceremony, which took place in the Throne Room of Government House, was 'not imposing', Lady Dufferin wrote. Just a few gentlemen standing around, and 'D.' signing a warrant, seated for the occasion on 'such a funny little throne with no back'. Their new residence was imposing alright, but uncomfortably so – 'gigantic with *no* room in it'. So Lady D. (as she was often called) at once moved her family into the visitors' wing where she discovered a pleasant boudoir for herself; it overlooked the garden's palm trees and lawns and she had it done up in pink silk. The family breakfasted on its balcony each morning, 'while the green parrots and the crows look down upon us from the capitals of the pillars that support the verandah roof'. It was usually the only quiet interlude of the busy day, for soon the various aides-de-camp arrived to give advice and receive instructions.

Lord William Beresford was chief-of-staff, and 'from the highest military affairs in the land to a mosquito inside His Excellency's curtain, or a bolt on my door, all is the business of this invaluable person'. Under Lord William ranked the other A.D.C.s: Captain Harbord in charge of the kitchen; Captain Balfour who managed the music; Captain Burn for the invitations. Lord William, a devoted horseman, also superintended the stables and 'the turn-out' of the carriages in which the viceregal party rode, 'with four horses, postillions, footmen, out-riders and escort all in scarlet and gold liveries'. The khitmagars at table were similarly attired 'in long red cloth tunics, white trousers, bare feet, white or red or gold sashes round their waists and white turbans. The smarter ones have gold embroidered breast-plates and the lower ones have a 'D' and a coronet embroidered on their chests.'

Those hot and unremitting colours, significant both of imperial splendour and oriental magnificence, flashed again and again before the Dufferins as they pursued their dutiful rounds. They predominated at the first meeting with the Maharajah of Jodhpore, for whose reception a mile of scarlet cloth was laid. At its end sat 'D.', on a grand throne with large golden lions for arms; attendants with bunches of peacock feathers set in gold were ranged round him, and one had a white yak's tail in his hand, 'lest a fly should trouble His Excellency's composure'.

At the punctilious military parades the same colours flared – dashing crimson-coated cavalry on white horses; swirling russets of the Highlanders; phalanx of camels 'wearing smart red saddle-cloths and red Marie-Stuart caps upon their heads, with their ears coming coquettishly and becomingly out of them'; the golden glint of swinging mace and rod, bugle and trumpet as the bands marched by. Even at the many weary prize-givings of the various mission schools where, in spite of Mrs Steel's efforts, it was still customary to give a prize to everyone, the girls who curtsied before Lady Dufferin wore masses of gold bracelets and anklets, 'green and gold garments wound round with crimson muslins', white flowers in their elaborately plaited hair. 'None of the children really understand English,' she noted sadly. 'But they repeat "I Love Little Pussy" and "Mary had a little Lamb" in monotonous and tragic tones.'

The next line in her journal reads tersely, 'Lord Randolph Churchill arrived this evening'. For here was an occupational hazard of office in the 1880s and 1890s that earlier rulers had escaped – the frequent visits of various aristocratic, political or simply wealthy globetrotters who, since the opening of the Suez Canal route, included a 'cold-weather season in India' on their world tours. Lady D. was always discreet about her guests, but another memsahib, Sara Duncan, wife of a Calcutta journalist, was more outspoken on the theme. 'The genus globetrotter,' she says, 'is unloved in Calcutta.' Most particularly the 'Parliamentary globetrotter, who has given a character and finish as it were to the whole genus ... Regularly with December he arrives, yearly more vigorous, more inquisitive, more corpulent and more disposed to make a note of it. We have also noticed an annual increase in his political importance, his loquacity, and his capacity to form an independent opinion. At this moment we are looking forward to the last straw, in the shape of Lord Randolph Churchill ...'

Lord Randolph came, saw, made lots of notes undoubtedly and, during his stay at Government House, Lady Dufferin mentions, brought to lunch 'Sir Charles and Lady McGregor, Sir Auckland Colvin, the Marquis de la Grange and the Prince of Lucigne, Count de Fauciying', each equipped with 'piles of letters of introduction' to prominent Calcutta citizens. There was no recourse against the Letter of Introduction from Home, but for the unwelcome or over-persistent local caller, there was the defence of the Not at Home Box. Visitors asked the gatekeeper for the 'bokkus' and, if the mistress of the house was 'not receiving', they dropped their calling cards into it and drove off, often with relief, to the next house. Most memsahibs found the practice tiresome and silly because calls were customarily made at the hottest time of day and often by people of the merest acquaintance because convention demanded it. But the custom persisted – presumably because it gave callers a sense of mission and the called-upon a feeling of distinction.

Among the many who paid an extended call at Government House during the Dufferins' time were the Duke and Duchess of Connaught, who generated a non-stop whirl of activity wherever they went. Their three-day programme was a full one: first a visit to the Botanical Gardens, a polo match, the reception of 'a deputation of Mahometans'; followed by a 'small dinner of forty-three' in the evening; next morning before breakfast, a carriage ride to see a paper-chase with the Calcutta Hunt and 'all the hunters arrayed in the most sporting costumes', more polo in the afternoon and shopping in the bazaars and a State Dinner for seventy-three, then to the reception and buffet in the Marble Hall with 'many natives in fine dresses' among the guests. (Lady Dufferin was fascinated by formal Indian clothes and minutely details how this rajah wore a sage-green moire coat embroidered in silver, and that one's blue velvet waistcoats were trimmed with gold lace – but they remain picturesque oriental oddities with whom she seems to have had little verbal communication.) The Connaughts' next day began at 7.30 a.m. with military manoeuvres, a march past and a 'sham fight', followed by more shopping, a visit to Calcutta's Museum and a full-scale Ball for six hundred or so in the evening, with the royal pair leading off the first quadrille.

On the Saturday afternoon the Dufferins swept the Connaughts off to Barrackpore for a rest. The place that 'saved' Emily Eden from India retained all its charms fifty years later. 'We fell in love with Barrackpore on the spot,' wrote Lady D. as soon as she saw it, and, as it was now about an hour's train ride from Calcutta, the Dufferins went there most weekends. Picnic breakfasts under the famous banyan tree were a feature, and D. had a wooden-walled tennis court made between two wings of the house where 'several gentlemen in scarlet attend to pick up the balls'. The horticultural inspiration of several governing families had made the grounds 'quite perfect' by this time, Lady Dufferin decided. 'Roses in the greatest profusion, and some of them are quite enormous; the large blue convolvulus climbs all over along a low wall, which surrounds a little garden full of heliotrope and other sweet flowers, and where a little fountain plays in a marble basin; there are bushes of red and purple blossom and a lovely orange creeper covers the balcony near which I write . . .'

The green, home-like park contained the tomb of the 'gentle-hearted and noble' Lady Canning who died of fever during her husband's troubled period of office, and a Grecian-style military temple dedicated to the Memory of the Brave. Thirty-six elephants, appropriately fitted with scarlet and gold howdahs, were stabled in the back compound and were as spoiled as ever with buns, sugar lumps and chappattis spread with treacle. The Dufferins used sometimes to take a sunset ride on them to the riverbank, past the tank covered with red water-lilies, as George and Emily Eden once did.

Like the Edens too, the Dufferins were obliged to make their up-country tours – the first to Rawal Pindi and Lahore. Gone was all the slow and inconvenient business of herding thousands of cattle, horses, carts and people across un-bridged rivers or being 'doddled about' in a sedan chair before breakfast. The Dufferins simply boarded a train for forty-eight hours. And a 'perfectly delightful' journey it was – everything so fresh looking, no dust and no heat. Every station gay with welcoming flowers and, at length, 'glimpses of snowy peaks and trees in the foreground, all toned down by the recent rain into blues and purples and mysterious in-between tints'.

Gone too were all the minor discomforts of earlier days when gubernatorial entourages had provided only imperfect insulation from the rigours of the country. On reaching Rawal Pindi the Dufferins found that 'a whole town of tents' had been erected. Thirty-six, for the accommodation of themselves and staff, were arranged 'to form a street, eighteen on each side with a broad strip of grass in front of them and two wide roads with another wide stretch of grass down the centre, the length of which is broken with fountains and rockeries and ferneries. At the top of this double street is our tent palace . . . The first room in it is an enormous drawing-room, then comes a still bigger durbar tent and then – always under cover – you pass on to Her Excellency's boudoir, His Excellency's office, her bedroom, his room with dressing-rooms and bathrooms . . . And my boudoir opens to a square full of pots of flowers where a little fountain sprinkles a bed of maidenhair; and in all the rooms there are Persian carpets, sofas and armchairs; in the bedrooms, pier glasses, chests of drawers and wardrobes. The "street" has lamp-posts all down it and water laid on; there are telephones and a post office, messengers on camels and six extra aides-de-camp in waiting on us – and,' she concludes, 'that is the way we "rough it" in camp'.

After all that expenditure and effort, it is slyly satisfying to learn that the Indian climate was still able to make its presence felt. Torrents of unseasonable rain fell and chill winds blew fiercely under even the sturdiest canvas wall. The viceregal party sat huddled in shawls before sputtering charcoal stoves; servants bore the meals to them through 'seas of mud' that absolutely ruined their white trousers, and some of the minor dignitaries were 'washed quite out of their tents'.

In due course the weather improved and there were rounds of audiences for which the Dufferins donned all their finery, D. himself 'very gorgeous indeed in his Lord Lieutenant's uniform, the Star of India and the four collars of his various Orders ornamenting him richly both back and front'. The cream of north-Indian nobility was there, jewel-encrusted rajahs in pink, silver, purple, gold, turquoise, red, and the Amir of Afghanistan who made a little speech, as others had before him, about the friendship that existed between his country and England. He was accompanied by his state executioner 'who cuts off heads and hangs people when at home', but, being off duty, was all got up 'in red velvet and, wearing his axe and strangling rope, helps to put up the tents'.

When the grandest of all the grand durbars was over, the Dufferins, still in the tracks of the Edens, started towards Lahore and, as was customary, the gentlemen indulged in some hunting en route. To the ladies, as Lady Dufferin says, one day's shooting exactly resembled another, the only difference being in the quantity and variety of animals killed. The procedure was to ride elephants to some 'jungly region' where the local sports-loving rajah (often clad in hunting green) had prepared 'a series of arbours' for the viceregal party. When all were suitably settled and screened, 'silence prevailed and the distant sound of beaters broke upon our ears, and we looked with anxiety and excitement through the port-holes of our arbour'. That particular day was most successful; they counted thirteen species among their victims: 'several kinds of deer, sambar which is a very large one, cheetah which is spotted and has a fine head, wild boar, wild dog, foxes, jackal, hyena etc. The pig were very exciting and one nearly charged into our retreat.' But all was well and 'in the middle of the day we had lunch and between the beats we looked at all the dead animals and discoursed upon our adventures'.

On reaching Lahore, the Dufferins were entertained in the Shalimar Gardens – seventy acres of broad-walks, trees, fountains and waterfalls all illuminated with thousands of Chinese lanterns and wicks brightly burning in earthenware jars. There, also, was the tomb of Ranjit Singh whose remains were enclosed in white marble, topped with eleven marble knobs containing the ashes of the queens and slave girls burnt with him, a procedure of which Emily Eden had greatly disapproved at the time, in spite of her liking for the old man. And then, at long last, the Dufferins made for Simla, as people did when the stress of ceremonial and official life became too great.

During Lady D.'s first long season at Simla she started formulating plans for her famous Scheme, called 'The Countess of Dufferin's Fund for Supplying Female Medical Aid to the Women of India'. It does not sound much like her, but, in her published journal, there threads through all the scarlet and gold pomp a continuing undertone of genuine concern for the welfare of the unfortunate and disease-ridden ordinary people. Lady Dufferin's attention had been drawn to the plight of Indian women by Queen Victoria who had heard of their sufferings from some of the first women doctors belonging to the Zenana Mission Movement that had started in India during the 1870s. It was their accounts that prompted the Queen to ask Lady Dufferin if anything constructive could be done.

As Lady D. discovered, the religious laws of the land did not permit women in purdah (most of them Moslem, some Hindu) to be attended by male doctors. As Indian women doctors did not exist, this meant that purdah women in sickness or childbirth were left to the dubious and ignorant care of untrained dais (midwives) or others supposedly endowed with magical healing powers. The low-caste dais profession was hereditary, and mother passed on to daughter the secrets of such time-honoured skills as burning snake skins under the bed of a woman in difficult labour or plastering her uterus with cow-dung.

Rather than attempt to break down or even rapidly undermine the tradition-ridden bastion of purdah, Lady D. determined to recruit and train numbers of women as doctors, midwives and nurses who would be able 'to carry help and alleviation into the remote chambers of the zenanas and bibi-ghurs, behind whose jealously guarded doors no unrelated man might pass'. So, on a misty Simla August morning in 1885, she held a meeting about the scheme – 'a round table and pens, ink-bottles and paper, Sir Stewart Bayley, Sir Charles Aitchison, Dr Simpson, myself and Major Cooper all sitting round with our copies of the Prospectus'. Subscription lists circulated; Queen Victoria agreed to be the Fund's patron; Major Cooper, saddled with the honorary secretaryship, was bowed down with work. The following year, Lady D. had the satisfaction of laying the foundation stone for the first 'Dufferin Female Hospital for the Training of Women Doctors' in Durbhanga, where the local maharajah had agreed to provide most of the money.

The Scheme itself gathered momentum during Lady Dufferin's term of office and so did its essential premise – that Indian women were in very urgent need of women doctors. These were not easy to recruit, for Englishwomen themselves had not yet won their battle for admission to medical studies on the same terms as men. It was in order to open the medical field to all competent students, regardless of their sex, that the London School of Medicine for Women was founded in the 1870s. One of its most famous students was Miss Edith Brown, the daughter of a Whitehaven bank manager, who qualified as a Doctor of Medicine in 1891 when she was twenty-seven years old.

Immediately she had completed her training, Edith Brown, who had received a devoutly Protestant upbringing, set sail for India under the auspices of the Baptist Zenana Mission. Zenana Mission work was educational, medical and evangelistic, and was intended to reach and help the women of the East who were barred from any sort of contact with white male missionaries. It also gave strong-minded women a rare opportunity to organize things in their own way, for invariably, in a mixed-sex mission, the men were in charge.

There were several other missionary ladies on the ship in which Edith Brown travelled and, as was customary, they devoted most of the time to spiritual activities – prayer meetings, Bible-readings, hymn-singing and special services for those members of the crew who were 'insufficiently aware of Christ'. Among the missionaries was another young doctor, Ellen Farrer, and she and Edith Brown were the first two doctors sent to India by their society. When they landed at Bombay, Edith and Ellen went by train to north India; the former to Ludhiana, the latter to Bhiwani, a town on the plains about forty miles from Delhi.

The two women were of different temperament and did not always agree. Edith Brown was the more enterprising and dynamic and later became quite famous in missionary circles; Ellen was steady, persevering and stayed where she was put. The morning after she arrived at the Bhiwani Baptist Zenana Mission in November 1891 she opened the doors of the dispensary to her first patients, and she was still working there – in a larger, modernized building – thirty-five years later.

There were just three of them at Bhiwani in those early days: Isabel Angus, who had opened the Mission four years before, her assistant, Annie Theobald, who taught in the little school and, now, Ellen Farrer, who had no medical assistants or other nursing help. She prepared all her own prescriptions and dressings, and a Bible Woman with a stronger stomach than most kept her patients under chloroform while she was operating. At first several of the visitors to her dispensary ran away in fear the moment Ellen opened her instrument case, but as news of her medical skill spread, the queues lengthened at the door each morning and her days became ever busier.

Dr Farrer briskly summarized each one in a neat small hand in her neat small diary and has thus left a record of the typical life – its tedium and tiresomeness, the unquestioning and total acceptance of duty and service. 'Dispensary as usual today. Only ten patients . . . Old woman with ear trouble returned for more medicine . . . Sterilized instruments; running short of carbolic spray. Where *are* the supplies from Bombay? Munshi (teacher) came as usual after prayers . . . Got my bed curtain up at last then sifted rhubarb through muslin while Isabel read aloud from *Abraham Lincoln* . . . Opened nasty abscess on groin under chloroform and scraped it . . . Black ants everywhere just now . . . Isabel brought in baby with bronchitis; it looks very wizened and may be going in for smallpox too . . . Owe Annie three envelopes. Woman with dropsy arrived from Dadri on a camel. Cut orange peel for marmalade; Annie made it . . . Went to see the postmaster's daughter this morning, she has hysterics. Nice little Bible reading tonight on "Stillness for Service" . . . Cataract patient very sick all day, I don't know why. Thirty-five patients at Dispensary this morning, the most yet. My box of summer clothes arrived at last – half of them mildewed . . . Child with broken femur improving. The munshi very impatient with me today . . . Operated for removal of large warty growth from the vulva. Snake killed in Annie's bedroom. Order surgical scissors from Bombay. Three of the in-patients have low fevers and quinine doesn't seem to help . . .'

Then Ellen herself caught fever and quinine did not help her much either, so she went on a short tour of recuperation and evangelism with Isabel Angus – who describes it for the benefit of the homebound readers of the Baptist Missionary Herald. 'A February morning in an Indian village. The air is sharp, but the pale blue sky and bright sunshine promise a milder temperature and more settled weather than is likely to fall to the lot of folks in England. Smoke hangs over the thatched cottages and mud houses of the village. At a little distance, such as the laws of health demand, stands our small tent – dwelling house, dispensary and schoolroom for the time being. Some of the villagers presently find their way to the tent door, among them a woman who has often listened to the message of the Gospel and has for long appeared to be a seeker after God. It is, as she said to a relative with her, "Two years ago you remember that I sought after the other Way and was much taken up with the thought of it; but no help or salvation ever came from Krishnu. Now I have left that and am trying to understand this Way; but it is much more difficult." It seemed indeed difficult for her to comprehend how easy was the Way if she would but walk in it.'

So the three women kept going in Bhiwani, cheering each other with such tales of hopeful conversion, with hymn-singing and reading aloud, with making jam and cushion-covers – containing the country within familiar patterns of reference so that even the poverty-stricken, dusty Indian village could remind them of the thatched English countryside. Soon the remorseless heats came; Ellen donned her slightly mildewed cotton dresses. At the end of April 1892 she recorded that 'it was about a hundred and five degrees at about six p.m. and ninety degrees in the house'. A few days later she was again in bed with 'country fever', sewing an umbrella-cover to send to Mamma for Christmas, while Annie read aloud from *The Knight Errant* to cheer her up. The seasonal dust storms scourged the plains and in the middle of one a 'poor Brahmin lady with elephantiasis arrived' and then fled from the hospital in the night. The postmaster's daughter was safely delivered of a son, the woman from Dadri returned 'suffering from maggots', Ellen performed a successful cataract operation on a young girl, 'a very philosophic little mortal' who went home seeing and smiling after three weeks. At harvest times, the native women were forced to work in the fields however unwell they were, and few came to the Mission. At times of flood or famine they begged to be allowed to stay in the hospital for shelter and food. In general the work expanded and 'Sixty patients as usual today and did not finish till noon' became a common entry in Dr Farrer's diary.

The following summer there arrived letters from Dr Edith Brown, then stationed at Palwal, thirty-six miles south-west of

Delhi, describing her proposals to establish a medical school where women missionary doctors could train Indian women as nurses and assistants 'in a proper Christian setting'. The very few medical schools in the country to which women were admitted were run by the government or in association with the Lady Dufferin Medical Fund, and Christian converts were not encouraged to enrol because they were regarded with deep suspicion by orthodox Hindu and Moslem women. Edith had discovered that there were a number of fairly well educated Christian girls who would be most suitable for medical training, but whose parents would not allow them to attend a mixed-sex college – which was against their notions of propriety – and where Christianity was not a major part of the curriculum.

In December of 1893 Edith Brown put her proposals to a meeting of women missionaries in Ludhiana, suggesting that the various evangelical societies working in the region combine their resources to start the first 'North India School of Medicine for Christian Women'. The project aroused some opposition initially – from Ellen Farrer among others, who feared that it was not practicable – but Dr Brown was very determined. She overrode all objections, started fund-raising, persuaded the Baptists to free her so that she could become the principal of the new college. They did so on the condition that 'if the Scheme falls through, we regard Miss Brown as still our Agent and expect her to return to work for our Society as the Committee may direct'.

The Scheme did not fall through. The Society for Female Education offered a disused school-building in Ludhiana – a town that was a centre for Protestant activity over forty years before, when Mrs Helen Mackenzie lived in the compound of the Presbyterian Mission while her husband raised a regiment. Donations came in from such various organizations as the Ladies Association of the Church of Scotland and the American Methodists; the London Medical School for Women sent textbooks and apparatus. As the College's founder, Edith Brown took charge of everything – the making of calico curtains with turkey-red borders for the students' dormitories, discussions with the University of Lahore about affiliation to its medical faculty, the purchase of a covered bullock-cart to carry the students to the teaching hospital in the rainy season, the setting up of auxiliary fund-raising committees in England, the hire of a harmonium for the Sunday evening hymn-singing.

The school opened in November 1894 with a staff of two teaching doctors and one matron, and with six girls enrolled for nursing; by the second session there were four doctors, and twelve more pupils taking the four-year medical assistants' course. The capable Dr Brown settled into her work as Principal: 4.15 a.m. start for private devotions, breakfast at five, prayers with the servants and the students before they went to the teaching hospital, which was strictly purdah. Studies began at six a.m. and continued, with breaks, until 6.30 p.m., at which time the girls could play tennis or walk in the grounds, then dinner, Bible-reading, prayers and bed at nine o'clock.

In spite of the emphasis on the Christian Way for the students, the missionaries did not unduly impose their religious beliefs on the patients. 'How often patients' prejudices have to be considered in hospital treatment,' Edith wrote. 'A woman may refuse to have her hair washed or an operation done on a certain day, as it is an "unlucky" day, and the date has to be altered. She may object to the colour of clothing offered and it has to be changed. White is disliked as the colour for widows and as rendering it much easier for them to be attacked by evil spirits; so all are dressed in coloured garments. A strict Muslim may object to having her ear syringed before sundown during Ramzan, and arrangements have to be made for her medicines to be given by night instead of by day ... We have as cook a Brahmin woman, who carries the food around to the patients, a nurse accompanying her to see that the right quantity and kind are given in each case. But the nurse must not touch it nor let her shadow fall on it, nor touch the cook's clothing as she is carrying it; otherwise the food would be defiled.'

By western standards, conditions in the hospital were unhygenic and chaotic, but Edith Brown had sufficient experience of India to know how much could be attempted. Women were allowed to bring their children into hospital with them and, as Dr Mary Roberts, a rather astonished visitor, noted, 'they are to be seen sitting on the floor beside the beds in the midst of a miscellaneous assortment of cooking utensils and supplies, for in the Hindu ward especially, many of the patients have their food prepared by relatives who "camp out" in the compound and do the cooking over their little charcoal stoves'. But, as Dr Roberts realized, 'the patients must be allowed to live pretty much in their own free and easy way, or they would be utterly unhappy. Rigid rules would mean empty beds, and one soon sees the wisdom of giving them such absolute freedom; for though I never saw a hospital half so untidy, neither have I seen patients more happy and contented. Most of them are genuinely grateful for what is done for them, and if anyone doubts the value of medical missions, they should go with the Bari Miss Sahib (Dr Brown) as she makes her rounds. Everywhere she is met by beaming smiles and a chorus of "Salaams". One need go no further to see that physical healing is the best way to win the people's hearts.'

For over thirty years Dr Edith Brown remained in Ludhiana 'winning hearts'. Her hair greyed and she twined it in a single braid round her head, she wore pince-nez, the skin of her angular frame became freckled and dried by the fierce Punjabi sun. In short, she looked the missionary lady she was; typical of many other devoted labourers in the same vineyard. They did much to alleviate the sufferings of Indian women at a time when few others felt sufficient concern to help. Busily involved in the daily working round, the women missionaries were not especially aware of the pressures towards social change that were beginning to be felt in the country, for they accepted its basic structures and tried to work slow reform within them.

Their methods aroused sharp criticism from some of course – from Flora Annie Steel for example, who wrote that she had 'no sympathy with zenana missions or zenana doctors. By their means we undoubtedly lessen the amount of suffering. But pain is Nature's strongest fulcrum and I firmly believe that, but for our well meant efforts to make seclusion more bearable, India would, by now, be half free of the curse of purdah.' Mrs Steel's point touched upon matters of principle that exercised the minds of all who wished to bring about changes in India – as Annette Ackroyd had discovered. The nub of the problem was how far the process of social and judicial 'progress' along western lines could, or indeed should, be taken before it too drastically changed or destroyed the existing structure of Indian society, and, ever since the furore over the abolition of suttee in the late 1820s, the position of Indian women had been emotive and crucial. Lady Dufferin was a firm believer in gradual enlightenment; at one 'zenana prize-giving' she noticed that the unmarried women of the house were allowed to watch the proceedings through a screen and commented, 'I was glad they were able to have this amusement, though I am not a great advocate for "progress" in such matters, for I think that Eastern women cannot be too slowly brought forward.'

She was often dismayed by the common Indian assumption that Westernization was a sort of package deal. On the occasion of another of those interminable girls' schools prize-givings she remarks that 'with education unfortunately comes a taste for English millinery and a departure from the good taste generally inherent to a national costume, and I could really *groan* when princess frocks, marabout feathers and other shabby finery are flaunted before me'. Taught to spurn their own native arts of delicate embroidery, the pupils were being introduced to 'the crochet and woolwork of which we are so heartily sick at home'.

Similarly, Indian boys were being introduced to the mysteries of western-style science, mathematics and literature and, in the opinion of many Anglo-Indians, were becoming too big for their shiny patent-leather boots as a result. For their new knowledge inspired some of them to test whether indeed, as Queen Victoria's proclamation had stated, natives 'were to be freely admitted to all ranks of government service'. Lord Dufferin, who arrived in India the year the first Indian National Congress was held, announced during his early period of office that he was in favour of giving 'a wider share in the administration of public affairs to such Indian gentlemen as, by their influence, their acquirements and the confidence they inspire in their fellow countrymen, are marked as fitted to assist with their counsels the responsible rulers of the country' – which did not sound as if he were exactly going overboard in the cause of Indian nationalism. Nor did he, for Lord Dufferin was responsible for a general slowing-down of the process towards liberal reform pursued by his predecessor, Lord Ripon, and this made him popular with the Home Government, much less so among Indian politicians.

It was Lord Ripon who tried to introduce into the constitution the controversial Ilbert Bill. Named after the legal member of the Council, Courtenay Ilbert, the Bill recommended that Indian magistrates who held office outside the big cities should be allowed to try Europeans in open court. The suggestion was vehemently opposed by the Anglo-Indian community, who booed Lord Ripon in the streets of Calcutta, and the press took up the row with enthusiasm. One of the letters on the subject that received much attention appeared in the publication *The Englishman* and was penned by Mrs Annette Beveridge. She wrote: 'I am not afraid to assert that I speak the feelings of all Englishwomen in India when I say that we regard the proposal to subject us to the jurisdiction of native Judges as an insult. It is not pride of race which dictates this feeling, which is the outcome of something far deeper – it is the pride of womanhood. This is a form of respect which we are not ready to abrogate in order to give such advantages to others as are offered by Mr Ilbert's Bill to its beneficiaries. In this discussion, as in most, *Il y a question de femmes* – and, in this discussion, the ignorant and neglected women of India rise up from their enslavement in evidence against their masters. They testify to the justice of the resentment which Englishwomen feel at Mr Ilbert's proposal to subject civilized women to the jurisdiction of men who have done little or nothing to redeem the women of their own races and whose social ideas are still on the outer verge of civilization.'

By the standards of the time the Beveridges were definitely progressive in their attitude towards Indians, several of whom they counted as friends, and they had always been uneasy about the extent of British authority over the country's affairs. Since their marriage in 1876, Henry had been exercising his portion of this authority as a District Judge in parts of Bengal, and Annette had adapted to her new role – as wife, housekeeper, bearer and principal educator of their growing family. In 1880 they were posted to Bankipur in Bahar, where they held their first International Evening Party which, wrote Mrs George Grierson who attended it, 'was quite new up here, though they have them in Bengal'. Hindus, Baharis, Mahommedans, Bengalis and Europeans were invited and separate tents were erected in the compound so that those whose creeds and castes were different could eat their own foods at separate tables. The entertainment provided was also suitably international: a display of ancient Persian manuscripts in one room, intervals of music from the local military band interspersed with the chants of some Tetera players fingering their stringed instruments on one verandah; on another, European curiosities such as a telephone and an electric pen. The occasion was a great success, though the English ladies expressed themselves almost overcome by the smell of sandalwood and rosewater. A journalist of the local newspaper wrote that 'to the whole assembly of guests, the ineffable grace of her manners and kind attention which Mrs Beveridge showed us all was highly gratifying'.

Mrs Beveridge was among the relatively few enlightened Englishwomen of the time who willingly entertained native gentlemen in her home, but she was not prepared to grant them magisterial authority over her or others of her sex. It was an anamolous position and one that brought her into unusual public conflict with her husband, who had been a stout defender of the Ilbert Bill from the first and was saddened by her opposition to it. But, she wrote firmly from England to him, 'except for your regret I cannot regret having written the letter to *The Englishman*. I think it very extraordinary that anybody should find fault with the calling . . . of a people uncivilized who care about stone idols, enjoy child marriage and seclude their women, and where, at every point the fact of sex is present to the mind . . . I call it uncivilized in any nation when I see two people together and the notion of their being a man and a woman is the first suggested by their manner, and not the more commonplace one (as in England) of *two people*.'

It is an interesting viewpoint: to justify the continuation of a racially prejudiced practice on the grounds of the sexual discrimination so openly enforced by the racially discriminated against! That this stand was made by a woman as intelligent and broadminded as Annette is understandable on two counts. Firstly, all well brought up Victorian memsahibs must have felt genuinely and profoundly shocked by the explicit sensuality of Indian religious culture. The polygamous Indian male, it seemed, practised the kind of uninhibited and promiscuous sexuality that they dared scarcely even dream about, and it was very frightening to imagine such a man having legal authority over them. Secondly, Englishwomen witnessed the severe oppression of their sex that permeated all strata of Indian life, and while some accepted it as being in the natural order of things, others were sickened and angered by it. These are points usually overlooked when the memsahibs are accused of being more hysterical and uncompromising than their menfolk in their opposition to the early attempts at racial integration.

But Annette, though thoroughly confirmed in her opinion, did not think it quite proper to speak again in public opposition to her husband. 'My darling, I hope and trust that you and I will not fall out on the native question,' Henry pleaded with her, and she conceded at once. 'Ilbert Bills and Babus shall not divide us,' as she put it. Indeed nothing would seriously divide them for their marriage was a rich and vital union, the central factor of their lives. And, even while they debated the merits of the Ilbert Bill, they were also eager to re-explore the depth of their own relationship.

During one of their enforced separations Henry asked his wife in a letter if she ever felt she would have had 'a more brilliant career' if she had not married. She considered it – back to that anxious time of her spinsterhood ten years before, that state of 'semi-suicide which I, in ignorance and enthusiasm was committing in Calcutta', days 'in which, like Dorothea, I longed to widen the skirts of light and in which I floated as it were in a tide of sympathy with those for whom I worked'. But all that, she concluded, was 'far away and unregretted. For if then I might have drawn a few souls with me nearer to the light and have cheered a few workers with fellowship and sympathy, now I am firmly welded into the great chain of life.' She was content to 'live in' her children and encourage their progress. And, 'For you and me, my dear husband, what can I say? I have no higher desire than to be loved by you, to make you happy and to see you honourable and honoured.'

So Annette entered no more into the arena of public debate and Henry, an honourable man, continued to express views about Anglo-Indian relations that were considered far too liberal by his superiors in the High Court. He was several times passed over for further promotion and when he retired from the I.C.S. in 1893 he was still in the Bengal backwoods, still a District Judge. By that time Annette had settled in England permanently with the children and, though she missed India, she did not find separation from it so very painful. She never really forgave the country for so shattering her early impulsive idealism, for teaching her the bitter lesson that the ways of the East could not be easily altered, even by one possessed of her courage and enthusiasm.

Chapter Twelve

Ten years after Queen Victoria's assumption of the title of Empress of India there was further occasion for celebration – her Silver Jubilee. In preparation for it, Calcutta, wrote Lady Dufferin, 'became a city of bamboos. Every house in the place is caged by scaffolding preparatory to the illuminations ... Our house and all our gutterings are framed with bamboo spars and our dome is ribbed with rows of lamps; little saucers for oil are all the way round the top of the house and men are kept there to watch over them, as the crows and hawks knock them down.' Jubilee Day began with a salute of a hundred and one guns and a grand march past the crowded Calcutta maidan. At the service in the cathedral, 'the Bishop spoke with great feeling of the Queen'; in the afternoon Lord Dufferin held an immense levee on the race-course and, when darkness fell, every saucer of oil round the top of Government House was lit and there was a most splendiferous firework display: 'The Queen's portrait, those of the Prince and Princess of Wales and our own appeared out of a great bunch of roses and thistles which faded away leaving the picture in outline.' The crowds gasped in awed delight and the whole affair, Lady Dufferin concluded, 'has been a magnificent popular fête. No accident has marred its complete success.'

And so India's Empress in distant Balmoral and her viceregal representatives in Calcutta were set fair for another spell of imperial peace and practically unequalled prosperity – though most Anglo-Indians failed to appreciate this. Indeed they grumbled, as they always had, that the most glorious days of Empire were already over. 'The age of the Nabobs is truly past, the Pagoda Tree is extinct as the dodo,' Mrs Steel claimed in the preface to the third edition of her housekeeping book. Prices had risen shockingly since she wrote the original, and 'though butcher's meat is still cheap and the cost of the necessities of life are reasonable, the rupee at one shilling and fourpence makes economy a grave question for most Indian officials'. Bearing which in mind, Flora draws her readers' attention to her thrifty recipes using home-grown vegetables and hints on the management of khitmaghars' wages.

House prices had increased too and one traveller who visited Bombay in the late 1880s was dismayed to find that 'the British residents, supposed to be lords of the city, have no place to live in. Our rule has enriched the natives till they outbid us for the luxuries and even the necessities of life.' The over-enterprising Parsees were specially guilty in this respect, buying up all available land, and the only remedy would be to 'mark off reservations in all large cities to be occupied by Europeans only'. Even job promotion was by no means a certainty any more, for 'Eurasians and educated natives now compete with Europeans for vacant offices', and one had to be very careful not to let them get ahead.

However, these portents of things to come, like the first mutterings of Indian nationalism, did not seriously disrupt the crystallized rhythms of the high Raj. Commissioners, maharajahs, colonels and their ladies came and went through the stately portals of Government House, feeling their future secure, and the Vice-reine dutifully opened more orphanages, visited missionary outposts, inspected schools and patronized charitable Fancy Fairs. These fairs were a feature wherever several memsahibs gathered together and the report of one of them, given in the Calcutta *Morning Post* of March 1887, suggests why all the top mems. from Lady Lawrence to Lady Dufferin, contemplated their arrival with a resigned sigh. 'There were four stalls tastefully arranged in Morrison's verandah, each little "boutique" was divided from the other screens, and all the latest novelties in art and fashion were on display. Mrs Dubisson, surrounded by a bevy of fair attendants [presumably no pun intended] sold everything from a needle to an anchor. Next to her was Mrs Hutcheson's stall where numerous raffles of Lucknow and Cutch silverwork created great excitement. The third stall was kept by Lady and Miss Edge whose gold and silver embroideries were very fetching . . . Mrs Thompson presided over a charming bon-bon and sweetmeat tent and Mrs Bradshaw dispensed tea and coffee... Mrs Tarley's waxworks were a great feature in the day's programme; Miss Colvin as the Queen of Hearts was a real picture. The receipts of the Fair, after all expenses had been paid, amounted to Rs. 6,000 – a very handsome addition to the Ramsey Hospital Fund.'

In due season the heats arrived, charitable enthusiasms waned, the woven-grass blinds of Government House were drawn down tight against the blaze of the Bengali sun and the viceregal family left for the hills. Their courtly and indirect progressions took them through some of the places where, thirty years before, the now almost unbelievable battles had been fought. At Lucknow the bullet-pocked ruins of the Residency and its adjacent buildings had been left standing and had acquired, over the years, a patina of picturesque, half-legendary fame. Lady Dufferin was taken on a guided tour by General Wilson, a siege survivor who had helped to hold the Bailey Gate where Katherine Bartrum had once watched anxiously for her lost husband. Lady Dufferin was shown the underground rooms where Adelaide Case and Julia Inglis spent so many fear-racked hours, and the room where Sir Henry Lawrence received his death wound. After the Mutiny the jumble of bazaars close to the Residency boundaries had been demolished and a thoroughly English-style order imposed upon the rebellious city. 'It seems to be one of the nicest stations in India,' declared Lady Dufferin. 'There are great open park-like spaces, intersected with broad roads over-shadowed by fine trees, and all the grass, shrubs and leaves are so green and luxuriant-looking compared to other places. The bungalows all have nice gardens and the whole place looks as well-kept and rich and neat as a gentleman's park at Home.'

Cawnpore, on the other hand, remained as unlovely as ever – harsh, gritty, dispiriting. According to a contemporary guide-book, it had been the scene of 'an encounter between Europe and Asia more memorable than that of Thermopylae or Anabasis, as showing the characteristic results of different climates and different civilizations'. A Memorial Church had been built, its inside walls lined with engraved stone tablets, one of which read 'In Memory of Mrs Moor, Mrs Wainwright, Miss Wainwright, Mrs Hall, forty-three soldiers' wives and fifty-five children' – for, even in death, the 'soldiers' wives' remained nameless and of scant remark.

From the top of the 'Massacre Ghaut', Lady Dufferin could 'see the ravine down which the victims toiled in the hot sun and could imagine the boats grounding on the sand and the treachery that awaited them at the water's edge'. The 'saddest spot of all' was the Memorial Well in the Memorial Gardens. It had been filled in, surrounded by an ornamental wall, in the centre of which was carved 'the white marble figure of an angel. She leans against a cross and has long wings touching the ground; . . . We did not think her face quite beautiful enough, but the whole suggests sorrow, silence and solemnity and so far is successful. No native is ever allowed to enter this enclosure and they have to get passes to come into the Garden.' There was a division of opinion, she added, on the subject of these painful memorials. Some Anglo-Indians felt they were inappropriate for the peaceful times; others maintained that 'we should not let the people imagine we have forgotten what happened'.

From Cawnpore the Dufferins went by train to Simla, that ultimate eyrie to which, for the last half century, the British had flown in order to escape from and forget what had happened, or might yet happen in the 'real India' of the plains. Ever since Emily Eden had pronounced that Simla was the one place in the country worth the trouble of getting to, the ruling Anglo-Indian families had found it attractive and contrived to spend more time there. It was John, now Lord Lawrence who, when he was Viceroy in 1864, first made Simla the seat of government during the summer months – a period that was gradually extended from April to October.

In Lawrence's time, viceroys were housed in a rather unimpressive edifice called Peterhoff, that did not measure up to the more ambitious life-style of his successors. Lord Lytton, with his love of the grandiose, called it a 'sort of pig-sty'; the private chaplain of Lord Ripon decided it was more like a shooting-box; Lady Dufferin, when she first saw the house thought of it 'as a cottage and very suitable for any family desiring to lead a domestic and not an official life, but very unfit for a Viceregal establishment. Altogether it is the funniest place! At the back of the house you have a yard of space before you tumble down a precipice and in front there is just room for one tennis court before you go down another.' In fact, all Simla struck her as being precariously perched and rather primitive – even though it had expanded considerably since the Edens' time, with several European shops, three banks, a club and four churches. But still, Lady D. wrote, 'the aides-de-camp are all slipping off the hill in various little bungalows and go through the most perilous adventures to come to dinner. Walking, riding, driving all seem to me to be indulged in at the risk of one's life and even of unsafe roads there is a limited variety.'

But she soon got a grip on the place. As Number One Memsahib, she was allowed to ride in a carriage along the main thoroughfare, while everyone else had to use a rickshaw or 'dandy' (a sort of litter). Where wheeled vehicles could not pass Lady Dufferin rode a mule called Begum, a beast with 'a reassuring look in her eye' who went through streams and up narrow mountain paths 'without ever slipping or seeming to think it at all extraordinary'. She soon decided that Peterhoff must be abandoned before it fell off one precipice or other under the weight of their elaborate social entertainments, and she persuaded D. that the Home Government must finance the construction of a Simla residence more capacious than any former ruler had enjoyed.

So, on the summit of Observatory Hill, the new Viceregal Lodge came into being, and the Dufferins moved in during 1888, the last year of their office. It was a fitting backdrop for the imperial scenario: built of grey stone, adorned with wide pillared verandahs on two levels and a corner tower. Its huge drawing-room was furnished in brown and gold silks by Maples of London; the more sombre dining-room was panelled in teak, 'along the top of which are shields with the arms and coronets of all the Viceroys and of the most celebrated Governor-Generals'. There was even an indoor white-tiled laundry and Lady Dufferin wondered whether the dhobies would ever get used to it as an alternative to squatting beside a stream, 'there to flog and batter our wretched garments against the hard stones until they think them clean'. More innovatory yet was the installation of the most marvellous of modern miracles – electricity. 'The lighting up and putting out of the lamps is so simple that it is quite a pleasure to go round one's room touching a button here and there and to experiment with various amounts of light.'

So Simla remained as it had ever been, a place where the lights never went out and the voices of the British 'heaven-born' and their mates continued to tinkle down its hills from the time of Emily Eden to the end of the century. For most people there was little to do but play games. Archery contests were an early craze and the ladies' arrows zipped purposefully through the air of picturesque Annandale glade. When croquet came into fashion, Lord Lawrence proved something of an expert and the ladies gasped with admiration at his skill. During the 1870s, lawn tennis superseded other sports and courts were laid on every square of level ground, upon which the black-faced monkeys used to gambol in the early hours before the later players arrived. 'Bright-faced and neatly dressed girls come out arrayed for the combat,' recorded C. T. Buckland, and 'those who are accustomed to judge Indian ladies only from their pale and worn countenances when they return invalided to England would hardly believe with what vigour and spirit the ladies play lawn-tennis in India as long as their health and strength lasts'.

By way of change there was football, cricket, clay-pigeon shooting and tent-pegging for the young men, tilting the ring for the young ladies who, Lady Dufferin remarked, loved to go 'galloping about, lances in hand, their hats falling off, looking very energetic and very much amused'. It was all good clean competit-ive fun – polo-matches and gymkhanas, horse- and dog-shows, postillion races, steeple- or paper-chases and rickshaw-races, invariably won by those ladies most competent in the art of 'directing their men when to spare themselves and when to strive'.

Sometimes the British parodied their own competitiveness, as in the annual Victoria Cross Race, for which event, Lady Dufferin wrote, entrants were each equipped with life-size dolls that had to be rescued 'from the scene of battle. Some were in uniform, one was an Ayah' and Lord William Beresford (always the life and soul of any equestrian event) sported a 'Special Correspondent'. First the riders carried their dolls 'to a certain part of the field where they strewed them about like wounded men. Then they went back to the starting post and galloped to the figures; each man dismounted, picked up his doll and flew back. Lord William was first, but unluckily in jumping the last hurdle he hit his head against a post . . .' and was led from the field, clasping the Special Correspondent in his arms to staunch the blood.

The British penchant for dressing up and guying both themselves and 'the natives' was given its head at the popular Fancy Dress Balls. At one of the first to be held in the new Viceregal Lodge, the Commissioner of Assam appeared as a Manipur chieftain, an aide-de-camp's sister came as a Brilliant Gadfly, Lord William, recovered from his fall, but 'hobbling on a stick and coughing painfully', was 'the most perfect Chelsea pensioner', and D. himself was so cleverly disguised as 'an Arab gentleman' that even his wife did not recognize him. Ladies and gentlemen with real theatrical flair took to the boards of Simla's new Gaiety Theatre, which opened in the mid-1880s with a première of *Time Will Tell*. It was a comedy-farce, as were most of the theatre's early successes, such as *The Money Spinner, Ali Baba, Bluebeard Re-trimmed*.

Another Gaiety play of the time was a burlesque of *Lucia di Lammermoor*, for which Miss Kipling, dressed as a nurse, read a prologue written by her brother Rudyard. For Rudyard Kipling made several visits to Simla at the time and appeared in the cast of *A Scrap of Paper*, a comedy performed at Lady Dufferin's request to raise money for her medical aid fund. The cause presumably won Kipling's sympathy, for, when the Dufferins were about to leave the country, he wrote *The Song of the Women*, a lament supposedly uttered by all those ailing Indian females who were, he imagined, convulsed with gratitude by Lady Dufferin's efforts on their behalf. The first of several verses reads:

How shall she know the worship we would do her?
The walls are high and she is very far.
How shall a woman's message reach unto her,
Above the tumult of the packed bazaar?
Free wind of March, against the lattice blowing,
Bear thou our thanks, lest she depart unknowing . . .

It was actually in December of 1888 that the Dufferins left India, treasuring every moment of their last sun-warmed breakfasts on the Government House verandah among the parakeets and 'shuddering at the thought of London fog'. Lady Dufferin's last public function was the laying of a foundation stone for the Lady Dufferin Zenana Hospital in Calcutta, on which occasion she was presented with yet another golden trowel.

But the efforts of Lady Dufferin and other less notable Englishwomen of equally good intent were little recognized at the time – when Rudyard Kipling was busy fashioning his image of the typical hill-station memsahib. For she was frivolous, vain, sometimes adulterous, a heartless bitch with an ever-tinkling laugh and the occasional soft spot for a handsome subaltern. The qualities that Kipling most admired – courage, resolution, a dogged devotion to duty – were those born of imperial necessity and were, in his view, essentially masculine; the imperial challenge was, to him, a proving ground for young men only. His womenfolk, though allowed a certain cleverness and wit, were invariably poor creatures compared to the heroes of Empire, whom they were lamentably prone to distract from life's sterner duties. It is unfortunate that Kipling did not broaden his canvas to include as much diversity of character among them as he developed for his male characters, because it is his stereotyped and superficial version of the nineteenth-century Anglo-Indian woman that has remained current ever since as being truly representative of the whole species.

A few years after Kipling had made his literary name, Maud Diver made a plea for 'a more sympathetic understanding' of the Englishwoman – on the grounds that she was very much a helpless victim of adverse Indian circumstance and that the 'random assertion' made by Kipling and his imitators about 'the lower tone of social morality' in India was 'unjust and untrue'. According to Mrs Diver there were several temptations for the average memsahib that were more frequent and vitiating than any light leap towards occasional infidelity. For instance, 'that insidious tendency to fatalism – to accept men and things as they find them without enthusiasm and without criticisms – which lurks in the very air they breathe'. Allied to this, 'an astonishingly rapid waste of nerve tissue, due to the climate and the artificial shifting about life that she leads', which, in turn, produced 'a restlessness and irritability in certain temperaments, and in others that curious slackness – mental and moral – of which the Anglo-Indian woman stands accused'.

Having said so much in extenuation of her 'exiled sisters' however, Maud Diver has to admit that their behaviour is not always blameless, especially when they were taking the mountain air and away from their husbands' protective custody. 'The proverbial relation between Satan and idle hands is too often confirmed in the Himalaya, and for a woman who is young, comely and gifted with a taste for acting, Simla is assuredly not the most innocuous place on God's earth. Here frivolity reaches its highest point, and social pleasures are, to all appearance, the end and aim of everyone's existence.' Was it any wonder then that 'lightly dipped natures grow frivolous in such an atmosphere; that even the more seriously inclined succumb, for a while, to the irresistible charm, the lightness and brightness and irresponsibility of Anglo-Indian life'?

But what a delightful prospect that must have seemed to the majority of those potential memsahibs who, as Sara Duncan put it, frolicked eastwards during the last years of the century 'in excellent form for tennis, dancing, riding and full of a charmed appreciation of the "picturesqueness" of India'. Typically, Sara Duncan explains, such a one would have been well prepared for her new life, for India was no longer such an adventurous and incalculable terra incognita when Home contained numbers of safely retired ex-mems, with sun-dried cheeks and occasional yearnings for ripe mangoes, who delighted in giving advice to the young outward bound.

And so the travelling young lady would be bombarded with conflicting and intense directions about, for example, 'her shoes and slippers; it was impossible to get nice ones in India; they were made very well and cheaply in the China Bazaar; they lasted for ever if one took care of them; they were instantly destroyed by mould and cockroaches when the rains came. She would require a size larger than usual on account of the heat; she must remember to take a size smaller because she would use her feet so little that they would shrink.'

Young ladies determined to use their feet to the full could even go on hunting expeditions, as their brothers did. Isabel Savory, *A Sports-Woman in India*, found it novel and exhilarating 'to rove about in gypsy fashion, meeting with trifling adventures from time to time'. This sporting life was, she pointed out, 'a complete change for an ordinary English girl; and it is very easy to find every scope for developing self-control and energy in many a tight corner'. She experienced, and breathlessly wrote up, her share of tight corners while shooting three tigers in the Deccan, black bear in the Himalayas and sticking pigs in the Punjab. She also offered advice to other sportswomen about the safe handling of bamboo spears while riding side-saddle, the wearing of dogskin gloves in order to hold rifle barrels in burning temperatures, the steps a lady should take if she happened to meet a wounded leopard.

And so the young women travelled, equipped as for a continuous festival of imperial celebration; their huge cabin-trunks, crammed with garments suitable for every possible contingency of climate and circumstance, were humped from one end of the the country to the other. In their hot hands they clutched guidebooks which reassured them that it was possible for any 'British tourist in good health' male or female, to 'do' thoroughly India without going more than fifty miles from a good railway station. So many 'spins' arrived that none could count on having the choice of three regiments as in Emily Eden's day, or even an elderly colonel waiting for every cotillon. Competition for those eligible males of the I.C.S. with their promotion prospects and pensions was also tougher than it used to be, and, in short, reported Isabel Savory, 'the palmy days for the women have followed in the wake of other "good old days". It is so easy to run home on three months' leave – every subaltern does it; it is so easy to run out from England – every wife and sister does it; and thus it comes to pass that there is nothing new under the sun; that matrimony, when so much choice is available, can no longer pose as an unknown and intoxicating paradise'.

Not that, Isabel hastens to add, all young women went to India simply to find husbands anymore. 'Every year women come out who travel over the globe with the object of seeing other sides of that interesting individual, man, other corners of the world, other occupations and other sports – women in short who will enjoy a little discomfort for the sake of experience.' Some of them belonged to the relatively new breed of single career women who, still very rare in Annette Ackroyd's days, were beginning to take a more active professional part in the hoped-for modernization of India by working there as doctors, missionaries, teachers. They were usually serious and high-minded, determined to 'improve India' (by which they meant making it more like Home) and some of them reached a deeper understanding of the people by working with them, as only Anglo-Indian men had done in the past.

The rapid development of rail and road communications meant that the Anglo-Indian women were more mobile, less at the mercy of the country, less likely to vegetate in some remote out-station bungalow for months on end. The invention of electricity made for improvements in housekeeping methods, and new medical discoveries made them less susceptible to the illnesses that had carried off so many young Europeans in the past. The gradual broadening of educational and social opportunities for women in England was reflected, to some extent, in Anglo-Indian community life. It was now quite permissible to start schools for Moslem girls or charity funds for Hindu widows; to teach English, go on tiger-shooting expeditions, take up nursing or Indian archaeology.

An insufferable but long-experienced commentator on the Calcutta scene wrote of the 1890s that 'the present race of the fair, dear and charming companions of our life in Hindustan are happily far from having anything in common with the lolling, vapid, washed-out, poor useless creatures most of their predecessors in old Anglo-Indian times certainly were. Thank heavens! Those dear ones are now too imbued with the Home-English feeling of independence, are much too spirited and fond of healthful excitement to permit them ever to subside into the luxurious and slothful habits of the poor native harem ladies' – or the lackadaisical ladies of yesteryear.

But many of those ladies of yesteryear – the lackadaisical and the adventurous, the tough and the timorous – were founders of several generations of Anglo-Indian familes who, by the 1890s, could proudly number among their forbears soldiers killed in the retreat from Kabul, government officers who had known the famous Lawrences and had their share of Punjabi headaches, grandmothers who had survived the siege of Lucknow, or aunts who had died in childbirth in a moffusil bungalow. They could count among their living relatives a cousin or two in Calcutta, an uncle in Bombay, a brother serving in a Native Infantry regiment, a sister married to a District Judge. For those born into such families, India was expected destiny and, as Maud Diver points out, 'more than half the Anglo-Indian women in India today [1900] have spent their girlhood and early childhood in the country – which in most cases means that they have been sent Home at the age of seven or thereabouts, returning at seventeen to face the chief business of their lives . . .'

And that was to be a memsahib – to bring up a brood of pale-faced, reputedly rather spoiled and listless children; to deal with ayahs and wet-nurses, cooks and gardeners; to pay duty calls, give supper parties, organize stalls for Fancy Fairs; to suffer under the remorseless sun of the plains, to escape joyously to the cool air of the hills. Thus, Maud Diver explained, the chapters of the average memsahib's career unfolded – as 'wife', 'mother in exile', 'hostess and housekeeper'; and she lived through them 'with a heart sobered by experience and self-knowledge . . . till the years of her husband's work are accomplished and it is she herself who must go, leaving the younger generation to tread the same paths and uphold the same traditions after their kind'. Mrs Diver's tone is inimitably high Raj: portentous and proud, snobbish and self-congratulatory, sentimental and self-pitying. We have learned enough since to dislike and distrust it. And yet, when all is said, the burden of the white woman in nineteenth-century India was seldom light, and she received scant praise for taking it up.

Bibliography

I. *Manuscript Sources*
i. Archives of the Centre of South Asian Studies, University of
Cambridge:
    The Diaries of Clementina Benthall (Benthall Papers, 1841–3)
    Regulations of the Queen's Military Widows Fund (Simla, 1873)
    Diary of Fanny E. Kingnett (Boileau Papers, 1857)
ii. India Office Library:
    Letters of Jane Maria Strachey (Strachey Papers, 1863)
    Diaries of Annette Beveridge (The Beveridge Collection, 1872–4)
    Letters of Mr and Mrs Sydney Terry (1844–47)
    Journals of Honoria Lawrence (The Lawrence Collection, 1837–46)
    Memoirs of Emily Theophilia Metcalfe (1895)
    Diaries of Mary Irvine (Wimberley Papers, 1835, 1837)
iii. The Baptist Missionary Society Library:
    Diaries of Dr Ellen Farrer (1891–93)

II. *Newspapers and Periodicals*
    'The English in India, Our Social Morality', *Calcutta Review*, 1844
    'Englishwomen in Hindustan', *Calcutta Review*, 1845
    The Times of India, May 1870
    The Morning Post, Calcutta, October 1890
    'Ten months Captivity after the Massacre of Cawnpore', *Nineteenth-Century Magazine*, May 1913
    'Through the Sepoy Mutiny', *Chamber's Journal*, 1931

III. *Published Books*
    Anglo-Indian Domestic Sketch Book, anon., London, 1841
    Atkinson, G. F., *Curry and Rice*, London, 1859
    Bamfield, V., *On the Strength*, London, 1974
    Bartrum, K., *A Widow's Reminiscences of Lucknow*, London, 1858

Beames, J., *Memoirs of a Bengal Civilian*, London, 1961
Bence-Jones, M., *Palaces of the Raj*, London, 1973
Beveridge, W. H., *India Called Them*, London, 1947
Braddon, E. N., *Life in India*, Calcutta, 1872
Brown, S. S., *Home Letters*, Calcutta, 1842
Buck, E. J., *Simla Past and Present*, London, 1904
Buckland, C. T., *Sketches of Social Life in India*, London, 1884
Case, A., *Day by Day at Lucknow*, London, 1858
Collier, R., *The Sound of Fury*, London, 1963
Cunningham, H. S., *Chronicles of Dustypore*, London, 1879
Cust, R. N., *Essays*, 1886
Diver, M., *The Englishwoman in India*, London, 1909
—— *Honoria Lawrence*, London, 1936
Dufferin, Marchioness of, *Our Vice-Regal Life in India*, London, 1889
Dunbar, J., *Golden Interlude*, London, 1955
Duncan, S. J., *Adventures of a Memsahib*, 1895
East India Sketch Book, anon., 1832
Eden, E., *Up the Country*, London, 1866
—— *Letters from India*, London, 1872
—— *Miss Eden's Letters*, London, 1913
Edwardes, H., and H. Merivale, *Life of Sir H. Lawrence*, London, 1872
Edwardes, M., *The Necessary Hell*, London, 1958
—— *Bound to Exile*, London, 1968
—— *A Season in Hell*, London, 1973
Emmanuel, L., *Jottings of a Bengal 'Qui Hye'*, London, 1898
Falkland, Lady, *Chow Chow*, London, 1857
Fitchett, W. H., *The Tale of the Great Mutiny*, London, 1898
Germon, M., *Journal of the Siege of Lucknow*, London, 1958
Indian Outfits and Establishments, London, 1882
Inglis, Lady J., *The Siege of Lucknow*, London, 1892
Jeffreys, J., *The British Army in India*, London, 1858
Keene, H. G., *Handbook for Visitors to Cawnpore and Lucknow*, Calcutta, 1896
Kincaid, D., *British Social Life in India*, London, 1973
King, Mrs R., *The Diary of a Civilian's Wife in India*, London, 1884
Lawrence, G., *Forty Three Years in India*, London, 1874
Mackenzie, H., *Life in the Mission, the Camp and the Zenana*, London, 1843
—— *Storms and Sunshine of a Soldier's Life*, London, 1884
Macrory, P., *Signal Catastrophe*, London, 1966

Maitland, J., *Letters from Madras*, Madras, 1846
Marriott, J. A., *The English in India*, London, 1932
Marryat, F., *Gup, Sketches of Anglo-Indian Life*, London, 1868
Morrison, J. L., *Lawrence of Lucknow*, London, 1934
Muter, Mrs D., *My Recollections of the Sepoy Revolt*, London, 1911
Osborne, W. G., *The Court and Camp of Ranjit Singh*, London, 1840
Paget, Mrs L., *Camp and Cantonment*, London, 1865
Parkes, F., *The Wanderings of a Pilgrim in Search of the Picturesque*, London, 1850
Postans, Mrs, *Western India in 1838*, London, 1839
Reynolds, C., *Punjab Pioneer*, Texas, 1968
Riddle, R., *The Indian Domestic Economy and Receipt Book*, Calcutta, 1849
Russell, W. H., *My Indian Mutiny Diary*, London, 1957
Sale, Lady F., *Journal of the Disasters of Afghanistan*, London, 1843
Speede, G. T., *The New Indian Gardener*, Calcutta, 1848
Steel, F. A., *On the Face of the Waters*, London, 1896
—— *The Complete Indian Housekeeper and Cook*, London, 1892
—— *The Garden of Fidelity*, London, 1930
Stocqueller, J. H., *Handbook to India*, Calcutta, 1844
Thomson, M., *The Story of Cawnpore*, London, 1859
Trevelyan, G. O., *Cawnpore*, London, 1859
Trotter, L. J., *The Earl of Auckland*, London, 1893
Waterfield, R., *Memoirs 1846–57*, London, 1968
Woodruff, P., *The Men Who Ruled India*, London, 1953

Index

Books of Related Interest in Century Classics

Letters From India
Lady Wilson

Introduction by Pat Barr

Lady Wilson spent 20 years in India from 1889 to 1909 as the wife of a civil servant. Written at a time when British women in India were taking a more active role in Indian life, these letters are valuable in that they reflect Lady Wilson's outward-looking and intelligent curiosity in her love for and understanding of the country and its people.

On A Shoestring To Coorg
An Experience of Southern India
Dervla Murphy

This popular travel writer finds in the tranquil mountains of Coorg—once the smallest province in British India—the only place outside Ireland she could imagine being a permanent resident.

The Waiting Land
A Spell in Nepal
Dervla Murphy

In 1965 Dervla Murphy braved bureaucracy, danger and squalor to help Tibetan refugees in Nepal. As ever, her surroundings, the people who befriend her, and her Tibetan mongrel, Tashi, captivate her and inspire her writing.

Where The Indus Is Young
A Winter in Baltistan
Dervla Murphy

The account of a journey with the author's daughter, Rachel, to Baltistan, also known as little Tibet. Undaunted by the onset of winter, they bought a pony for the six-year-old Rachel, and walked and rode through five valleys, including the perilous Indus Gorge. They met no other Westerners during their time there, and lived on the customary Baltistani diet of dried apricots. The adventures of this remarkable pair through a region containing the greatest concentration of high peaks in the world displays their ingenuity, fortitude and their sense of humour in the face of danger and discomfort.

Tales Of Travel
Marquess Curzon of Kedleston
Introduction by Peter King

Whether he is watching Sumo wrestling in Japan, under suspicion as a spy in the Pamirs or searching for a top hat in Persia, this pot-pourri of Lord Curzon's travel reminiscences will delight and entertain.

Full Tilt
Dervla Murphy

This highly individual account of Dervla Murphy's extraordinary bicycle journey from Dunkirk to India in 1963 is based on the daily diary she kept while riding through Persia, Afghanistan, over the Himalayas to Pakistan and into India. A woman traveller on her own with a bicycle (even with a revolver in her saddle-bag), in such hazardous countries still largely untouched by modernization, was an unusual focus of interest. Her resourcefulness matches up to her unexpected encounters, and the blind eye she turned on personal danger and her unselfconscious disregard of discomfort are remarkable.

Verandah
Some Episodes In The Crown Colonies 1867–1889
James Pope-Hennessy

A panorama of colonial life in several Crown Colonies during the last century, told as a biography of the author's grandparents. It was the extraordinary character of Sir John Pope-Hennessey's wife, Kitty Low, which prompted her grandson to immortalize them.

Every Rock, Every Hill
A Plain Tale Of The North-West Frontier and Afghanistan
Victoria Schofield

Victoria Schofield visited the North-West Frontier in 1979, before the Russians invaded Afghanistan, and discovered the attraction of a wild and beautiful land. The result is a carefully researched and well-written documentary on the North-West Frontier and the tribes beyond its borders.

A Ride To Kiva
Fred Burnaby
Introduction by Eric Newby

A paragraph in a paper caused Fred Burnaby to beg leave from his cavalry regiment in December 1875 to set out on horseback to Khiva braving the depths of the Russian winter. The book is filled with memorable characters, Cossacks, sleigh-drivers and Tartar horsemen.

When Men And Mountains Meet
The Explorers Of The Western Himalayas 1820 – 75
John Keay

The story of the quest for access to Central Asia and inland China through the formidable barrier of the Western Himalayas involved some characters as exceptional as the terrain through which they struggled.

A Princess Remembers
The Memoirs Of The Maharani Of Jaipur
Gayatri Devi and Santha Rama Rau

This is the story of the daughter of the Maharaja of Cooch Behar and widow of the Maharaja of Jaipur. Raised in a sumptuous palace staffed with 500 servants, she shot her first panther at the age of twelve, in later life won a seat in the Parliament of India with a staggering majority and has appeared on lists of the world's most beautiful women. Politically successful and a leading figure in India's women's movement, Gayatri's later life was marred by tragedies which are movingly described in this book.

Princess
The Autobiography Of The Dowager Maharani Of Gwalior
Vijayaraje Scindia
with Manohar Malgonkar

The widow of one of India's richest princes, Vijayaraje Scindia reflects on her former palatial lifestyle and her career as popular political leader.